essentials

Environmental Law and Policy

Editorial Advisors

Vicki Been
Elihu Root Professor of Law
New York University School of Law

Erwin Chemerinsky
Dean and Distinguished Professor of Law
University of California, Irvine, School of Law

Richard A. Epstein
James Parker Hall Distinguished Service Professor of Law
University of Chicago Law School
Peter and Kirsten Bedford Senior Fellow
The Hoover Institution
Stanford University

Ronald J. Gilson
Charles J. Meyers Professor of Law and Business
Stanford University
Marc and Eva Stern Professor of Law and Business
Columbia Law School

James E. Krier
Earl Warren DeLano Professor of Law
The University of Michigan Law School

Richard K. Neumann Jr.
Professor of Law
Hofstra University School of Law

Robert H. Sitkoff
John L. Gray Professor of Law
Harvard Law School

David Alan Sklansky
Professor of Law
University of California at Berkeley School of Law

Kent D. Syverud
Dean and Ethan A.H. Shepley University Professor
Washington University School of Law

Elizabeth Warren
Leo Gottlieb Professor of Law
Harvard Law School

ASPEN PUBLISHERS

essentials

Environmental Law and Policy

Jonathan R. Nash
Professor of Law
Emory University

Wolters Kluwer
Law & Business

AUSTIN   BOSTON   CHICAGO   NEW YORK   THE NETHERLANDS

To my parents, Ellen and Stanley,
who taught me the essentials, and
so much more.

Contents

CHAPTER 3

The Regulation of Air Pollution: The Clean Air Act 53

CHAPTER 4

The Regulation of Water Pollution: The Clean Water Act 75

CHAPTER 5

The Regulation of Hazardous Wastes: RCRA and CERCLA   97

Contents

Preface

What interests you about environmental law? It may be the location of environmental law at the confluence of many different interesting areas of study: politics, economics, law, science, and sociology. Few areas of law can boast such interesting policy questions and such a strong interaction between law and science.

It may be the interesting nature of the practice of environmental law. Environmental law rests on complex statutes setting out policy goals and rules, intricate regulations that elucidate and expand on the statutes, and case law interpreting the statutes and rules. It is a challenging, enjoyable area of law.

It may be that the practice of environmental law enables you to serve society and fulfill important societal goals. If detailed study of regulations makes environmental law sound somewhat dry (and it need not), then consider the important societal role you play when you use the law to protect human health and the environment. Indeed, even if you represent interests that are sometimes thought to be antithetical to environmental interests — think of representing corporations that conduct businesses that generate pollution as a byproduct — realize that you may be able to help the corporation "do the right thing" through your representation.

This book is organized to accompany you during your study of environmental law. It is primarily designed to augment a course that focuses on the pollution-control aspects of environmental law, as do (to my experience) most introductory survey courses in environmental law. These are statutory regimes, enacted by Congress and generally enforced by the Environmental Protection Agency (EPA), that are designed to regulate the generation of pollution in different media.

The book begins by discussing important fundamentals to the study and practice of environmental law. Chapter 1 discusses various justifications for environmental protection and raises important policy issues that go to the heart of the design of environmental laws. Chapter 2 provides an overview of two areas of law that are critical to understanding environmental law: constitutional law and administrative law.

Chapters 3 through 5 cover the major pollution control statutes: Chapter 3 discusses the Clean Air Act; Chapter 4 the Clean Water Act; and Chapter 5 the Resource Conservation and Recovery Act and the Comprehensive Environmental Response, Compensation, and Liability Act (which address the generation, treatment, and disposal of hazardous wastes on and in land).

Introductory environmental law courses often also include some coverage of statutes that seek to conserve natural resources. This book offers support in these areas. Chapter 6 discusses the protection of endangered and threatened species under the Endangered Species Act, and Chapter 7 addresses the important National Environmental Policy Act, which requires government decision makers to consider the environmental impact of government action.

The book concludes with overviews of two important areas of environmental law. Chapter 8 discusses the enforcement of the environmental laws, both by EPA and by private citizens. Chapter 9 discusses international environmental law, with a focus on its interplay and application in the domestic laws of the United States.

Although the book is designed to be used by students in an environmental law survey class, those studying natural resources will also benefit from much of the book's coverage. Chapters 1, 2, 6, 7, and 8 will all be relevant.

Finally, the book should be of use to students in areas other than those studying environmental law and environmental policy. In keeping with Aspen's Essentials Series, I have tried to write for an audience that has little or no background in law. Chapters 1 and 2 should be especially useful as an introduction to environmental law for non–law students.

I thank my wife Lori for her help and my son Theo for his support in preparing this book. I am also extremely grateful to the various editors from whose wisdom, suggestions, and care I benefited: Carol McGeehan, Taylor Kearns, Barbara Roth, and from Sylvia Rebert, project manager. The comments and suggestions of six anonymous reviewers were invaluable. Finally, I thank the students whom I taught at Tulane Law School, Hofstra Law School, the University of Chicago Law School, and Emory University School of Law; their comments and questions were immensely helpful as I thought about structuring and writing this book.

Atlanta, Georgia
March 2010

essentials

Environmental
Law and
Policy

understanding why environmental problems arise and why they need to be solved. With those frameworks in place, we will then turn to various possible justifications for environmental regulation. As we shall see, these frameworks and justifications suggest different forms for governmental intervention in matters environmental.

Before we delve into more technical consideration of frameworks through which we may understand environmental problems, let us begin by asking ourselves why we have concern about the environment. This question has many answers, and every person would probably identify several answers that explain his or her interest. That being the case, let us canvass a number of reasons.

First, you may be concerned with preserving areas of natural beauty and recreation. Many people enjoy visiting national and state parks. You also may benefit from areas of greenery and recreational opportunities closer to home.

Second, you may be concerned with conserving areas not because you, or someone you know, might like to visit them, but rather for their own sake. Consider that the steps one might take to vindicate this goal may be similar in structure to those one would undertake to vindicate the first goal, yet the policy justification in each case would be different. In the first case, one is interested in preserving areas for one's own benefit. This view, then, values the environment for utilitarian reasons and takes an anthropocentric — that is, human-centered — approach. In the second case, the interest is not utilitarian. What, then, underlies this interest? We shall consider this question shortly.

Note that this distinction extends to the goal of protecting endangered species. Some may think this goal advisable because a plant or animal species may provide the basis for a medicine in the future. Others may think that the species deserve protection in their own right or, to put it another way, that humans are not morally entitled to take steps that result in the eradication of species.

Third, your concern with environmental amenities and environmental problems may arise out of the distribution of those amenities and detriments. The wealthy and well-connected often enjoy the benefits of environmental protection while the poor and politically alienated do not; indeed, they often live in areas that suffer more heavily from environmental harms, perhaps because they need to live near the factories where they work. This concern, broadly referred to as *environmental justice*, also appears at the global level: Lesser-developed countries often have the worst levels of environmental quality, whereas developed countries are often responsible for more than their "share" of pollution output. Environmental justice is discussed in greater detail later in this chapter.

Fourth, you may be interested in stopping a human activity that may threaten the environment not because you are convinced that the activity will substantially affect the environment, but because you are not convinced that it will *not* substantially affect the environment. The available science may be too uncertain to guarantee a safe outcome. And you may think that a precautionary approach — grounded in some version of a *precautionary principle* — is advisable in the face of scientific uncertainty.

Fifth, you may be interested in protecting a human activity that will adversely affect some aspect of the environment not because you are particularly concerned about the immediate effects of the activity, but you believe that, ultimately, the earth is a unified system, and what may seem at first to be a small effect on one small aspect of that system may in the end throw the entire system into disarray. This understanding of *interconnectedness* advocates in favor of precautionary environmental protection.

As we turn now to our more detailed discussion of various frameworks to understanding environmental problems, it will be helpful to bear in mind the points on which we touched in this general discussion.

ECONOMICS AND ENVIRONMENTAL REGULATION

We begin with the importance of economic analysis to environmental regulation. This will strike some readers as odd, because many view the profit-centered mind-set of economics as entirely incompatible with, and opposed to, ecological concerns. However, to the contrary, economic considerations often argue *in favor* of environmental regulation.

Many environmental problems can be understood as examples of the *tragedy of the commons*. Developed conceptually by Garrett Hardin in the 1960s, the tragedy of the commons focuses on the problems associated with having resources jointly owned and the bad incentives that may arise from such "commons" ownership arrangements. The tragedy is well demonstrated through an example drawn from its original setting — a grazing area shared by owners of herds of cattle. Although each person privately owns all of his or her own head of cattle, they all own the grazing field jointly and enjoy equal, free access to it. The tragedy begins when one of the herders — say, Lori — realizes that she can sell more meat at market, and therefore make more of a profit, if she increases the size of her herd by one head of cattle. Because there is the same amount of grass available to feed even more cattle, the increase in the total number of head of cattle results in a decrease in the weight of each head of cattle. Still, Lori's profits increase: Even though each head of cattle in her herd weighs less than before, the total weight has increased by virtue of the additional head of cattle.

We thus see that Lori has benefited from increasing the size of her herd. Was any cost associated with this? We have already seen some cost: The size of each original head of cattle is less than it would have been absent the new addition. However, costs are also borne by the other herders: Each head of cattle in all the other herds will *also* weigh less than it would have absent

Lori's additional head of cattle. Notice, then, the imbalance between the benefits and costs: Lori enjoys all the benefits while the costs are borne not just by Lori, but by all the herders. In the language of economics, Lori has *externalized* some costs on the other herders.

Can we predict how the other herders will react to Lori's action? Each of the other herders may realize that he or she also can gain a benefit, while externalizing costs on others, by increasing the size of his or her herd. Let us say, in keeping with this logic, that every owner increases the size of his or her herd by one head of cattle. At the same time, however, for the same reasons as before, the weight of each head of cattle will decrease as additional heads of cattle are allowed to graze on the common grazing area. The result may be that, although each herder now has an additional head of cattle, the total weight of each person's herd nonetheless will be less by virtue of the (now substantial, by virtue of increase of one head of cattle per herder) total weight loss. If that is true, then each herder is worse off than he or she was before anybody increased the size of his or her herd.

If everybody is made worse off, then why will this tragedy ensue? The answer lies in the fact that, on our assumptions, each herder makes decisions for himself or herself and not for the group. If the interests of the group were decisive, then increases in cattle size might not occur. The problem is that, as we have seen, it was in Lori's personal interest to increase the size of her herd. And once she has done that, it is in everybody else's interest to follow suit.

This raises a question about Lori's behavior. Let us assume for the moment that Lori is open to considering how others will react to her action. If that is true, then even if increasing the size of her herd is in her short-term interest, she will foresee that others will follow suit, with the result that everybody — including Lori — will wind up worse off. Won't this be enough to deter Lori from increasing the size of her herd in the first place? The problem is that it takes only one cattle owner to "defect" from any agreement not to expand herds to give rise to the tragedy. Lori may be willing to forgo expanding her herd, but only if she is confident that no one else will take advantage of her goodwill: If Lori anticipates that Theo will expand his herd if she does not expand hers, then she may as well expand hers, too. Thus, again, absent an agreement among all the herders not to expand herds that everyone will respect, each herder has an incentive to expand his or her herd, even though in the end it is in everyone's interest not to do so.

Many unstated assumptions underlie this story. First, there is the assumption that economics motivates each actor. Put another way, everybody is concerned simply with obtaining as much wealth for himself or herself as possible. Although generally people are susceptible to economic concerns, it would be an overstatement to think that that is the case all of the time. Moreover, commentators have pointed to other societies with structures that value community over individual success. In such settings, the tragedy of the commons would seem less likely to occur.

A second unstated assumption is that the parties have not been able to reach an agreement that would restrict each person's ability to increase his or her herd. (Alternatively, even if some agreement in principle was reached, it has proven to be unenforceable.) In some ways, this echoes the first assumption, namely that each individual is concerned with his or her own well-being and not with the overall success of the community of ranchers.

A third assumption is that the resource in question — here, grazeable land — is scarce. If there were enough grazing land that Lori could increase the size of her herd without affecting the size of Theo's head of cattle, then there would not be an issue. The issue arises precisely because Lori's use of the resource conflicts with Theo's. As others have pointed out, scarcity becomes more likely to occur where markets and trading for goods have developed. Under those circumstances, incentives increase for individuals to use more of the resource than they need for their own personal consumption. This hastens the scarcity of the resource.

A final assumption is that technology does not evolve that allows the resource in question to go further. If it does, then the technological advance in effect staves off scarcity.

Despite the numerous assumptions underlying the stylized tragedy of the commons, the story generally rings true in many settings. Moreover, it has many applications in the area of environmental law and regulation. Consider, for example, regulation of fisheries. For generations, people have fished. Those who fish have enjoyed profit and, for a long time, did not have to worry about depletion of fishing stock. Over time, however, demand for fish grew. As a result, more people began to fish and, even more important, technology provided for larger boats and better nets that allowed each fisher to catch more fish — however, only if the stock of fish was large enough. When, over time, a fishery's stock of fish becomes depleted, those who fish have to compete to catch even fewer fish. In the long run, it would be in everyone's collective interest to catch fewer fish (or perhaps even to abstain from fishing); this would allow the stock of fish to replenish itself and then offer the promise of more fish to catch in years and decades to come. Yet the tragedy of the commons predicts that each individual fisher has an incentive to continue to fish and thus to externalize costs onto other members of society, who will have fewer fish to enjoy later. One can tell a similar story for other resources, including clean air and clean water.

How else might economics help us develop and refine environmental policy? Consider the desirability of evaluating possible environmental regulation by comparing the regulation's benefits to its costs. Indeed, so-called cost-benefit analysis[1] plays a large role in U.S. federal law. One variation of cost-benefit analysis — measuring cost-effectiveness — seems

defendant polluter could choose to pay the damages and then to continue polluting. To be sure, a court could try to order the defendant to pay the plaintiff so-called permanent damages — that is, not just the damages for injuries sustained to that point, but damages to cover all injuries into the future. The calculation of permanent damages is, however, challenging. This is especially the case when future injuries may include severe illness and even death.

Fifth, consider that nuisance law generally offers only relief ex post — that is, after a nuisance was already in effect. Under the *anticipatory nuisance doctrine*, courts are reluctant to order any relief based on a claim that an activity that has yet to begin will cause a nuisance in the future. This has substantial ramifications in the environmental context. Consider that environmental harms are often irreversible, catastrophic, or both. To ask a plaintiff to wait until environmental harm has actually occurred may be to ask the plaintiff to wait too long.

Sixth, consider the problem that arises with relying on judicial resolution of tort cases as a way to regulate environmental degradation. First, as we observed earlier, the resolution of cases in the environmental arena may often turn on complex issues of science. Judges (and juries) may be poorly positioned to evaluate scientific evidence. Second, a response that is substantially judicial will be piecemeal. Only plaintiffs who choose to bring suit will be represented, along with only defendants who are sued. This will preclude courts from fashioning broad relief. Courts generally are limited to resolving the interests of litigants who appear before them.[2]

Before we move on, we should note that the common law continues to play an important role in the evolution of environmental law. For example, *toxic tort* lawsuits still vindicate the rights of those harmed by toxic substances; these often take the form of class actions. Also, nuisance actions have been at the forefront (although generally not successfully) of the movement to regulate greenhouse gas emissions.[3]

THE DEVELOPMENT OF MODERN FEDERAL ENVIRONMENTAL LAW

Much of modern environmental law developed rather quickly, in the late 1960s and 1970s. Many statutes were enacted, and others were so substantially redrafted and expanded that it is almost as if new statutes were enacted.

The timing of the rise of modern environmental law coincides with the rise of the environmental movement. *Silent Spring*, a book by Rachel Carson that helped publicize the dire threat posed by pollutants on the environment, was published in 1962. Consider that the observance of Earth Day commenced in 1970. Particular episodes of environmental harm and contamination also focused public attention on the problem. The Love Canal groundwater contamination was a major factor in the quick passage of the Comprehensive Environmental Response, Compensation, and Liability Act (CERCLA) in 1980.

The form of modern environmental law is responsive to the shortcomings of the common law. As we shall see, modern environmental law generally takes an ex ante approach and favors administrative agencies over judicial adjudication. This is not surprising, in the sense that the failings of the common law made modern environmental regulation appropriate.

THE TOOLS OF MODERN ENVIRONMENTAL LAW

As noted earlier, modern environmental law takes a different approach from that of the common law. Modern environmental laws take the form of broad statutes enacted by Congress, as opposed to (at common law) statutes arising out of judicial decisions. These statutes take an overarching approach, as opposed to the case-by-case, piecemeal approach under the common law. They also generally impose ex ante requirements.

The legislature generally devolves authority to generate specific regulations onto regulatory agencies, such as the federal Environmental Protection Agency (EPA). (Other government actors — such as the Department of the Interior, the Army Corps of Engineers, the Fish and Wildlife Service, the National Highway Traffic Safety Administration (NHTSA), the National Oceanic and Atmospheric Administration's National Marine Fisheries Service, the White House Council on Environmental Quality, and the Bureau of Reclamation, as well as numerous state agencies — also play a significant role in environmental legal protection, especially on the natural resources side of the ledger. This book's focus on environmental protection means that EPA receives the most attention, although we shall discuss some roles played by the Army Corps, the Fish and Wildlife Service, NHTSA, the National Marine Fisheries Service, and state environmental protection agencies.) Given a charge, these agencies tend to develop considerable scientific expertise. When called on to review agencies' scientific determinations, courts in turn tend to be deferential.

On which tools does modern environmental law draw? Let us consider the options available to policymakers to achieve environmental goals. One option is simply to rely on an ex post system of liability. For all the reasons we have discussed previously in delineating the shortcomings of the common law to address environmental problems, such a system is unlikely to serve well, at least as a sole response. That said, at least one domestic federal environmental regime relies on an ex post liability system — the CERCLA regime, discussed in Chapter 5. In addition, a major principle of environmental policy (and especially of international environmental policy) — "the polluter pays" — is consistent with such a liability system.

Let us then restrict ourselves to affirmative tools that may allow a policymaker to achieve environmental regulatory reforms ex ante. One basic idea is to regulate pollution emissions.[4] This may entail regulating those who generate substances or products that ultimately create pollution, or, more commonly, it may entail regulating societal actors who actually generate the pollution. The latter form of regulation — that is, regulating those who generate the pollution based on their pollution output — is often called *end-of-pipe regulation*.

End-of-pipe regulation may take different forms. One option is to impose a limit on the amount of pollution that the polluter may emit per unit of product that the generator produces or to limit pollution output to a particular rate. Another option is to cap the total amount of pollution that the polluter emits over a given period of time.

Various methods are also available for setting the standard against which to measure end-of-pipe emissions. First, one may set the standard according to health considerations, perhaps also, with an eye to the precautionary principle, including a margin of error for safety. Second, one may consider the balance of costs and benefits of the standard, choosing the standard that maximizes the excess of benefits over costs.

Third, one may select simply a technology that all polluters must employ. A modified version of a *technology requirement* has the government select a technology, but then allows societal actors to achieve the pollution reduction that the technology achieves however they see fit, that is, either using the technology in question or in some other way. Note that these requirements can be based on existing technologies or can effectively demand the development of new ones; the latter category is often referred to as a *technology-forcing regulation*.

End-of-pipe regulations abound under domestic environmental laws. Most common are the effluent limitations imposed under the Clean Water Act and emissions limitations under certain provisions of the Clean Air Act. We shall discuss these in subsequent chapters.

Another regulatory tool is an environmental or pollution tax, sometimes also called a *Pigouvian tax* (after Arthur Pigou, an economist who studied and advocated such taxes). In its ideal form, the environmental tax is set at an amount exactly equal to the marginal harm caused by each pollution emission. The polluter then faces a choice when deciding whether to produce more widgets than it is already producing. The polluter may choose to produce an additional widget and to pay the taxes for the pollution it emits as a result. Alternatively, it may choose not to produce any more widgets and thus to save those tax dollars. The polluter also may choose to revamp the process by which it manufactures widgets so that less pollution is produced. That way, it may be able to increase widget production levels while reducing pollution output and thus also reducing the pollution taxes for which it is responsible.

The predicted result of an environmental tax is that polluters that face a marginal cost of pollution reduction that exceeds the tax will simply pay the tax. In contrast, those for whom the tax exceeds the marginal cost of pollution reduction will opt instead to reduce their pollution output. In this way, a tax can be expected to reduce some pollution output. Also, insofar as each actor decides on its own whether to pollute and pay the tax or not, a pollution tax regime affords flexibility to societal actors.

Pollution taxes have not been a popular regulatory choice in the United States, although at times they have been used under the CERCLA program. Pollution taxes have been far more popular overseas, particularly in the European Union.

Yet another regulatory tool is a system of marketable emissions permits, also sometimes called a *tradable pollution permit system*. Such a system arises in five basic steps. First, the government determines the relevant area or region to be regulated. This may be a metropolitan area, a watershed (in the case of water pollution), a state, a collection of states, or even the entire nation. Second, the government determines the level of pollution that can acceptably be emitted in any given year (or other relevant time period). Third, the government divides that total number into numerous permits, each of which authorizes the holder to emit a given amount of the relevant pollutant in a year. One may emit the pollutant in question only to the extent that he or she holds permits authorizing him or her to do so. Fourth, the government somehow distributes the permits to societal actors. This may be done by auctioning off the permits or, more commonly, by simply giving them at no charge to existing polluters in some proportion to their prior polluting activities. Fifth, the government allows free trade of the permits among societal actors.

A polluter subject to a tradable pollution permit system faces a choice. It may continue to produce widgets and pollute at the same level, provided that it has enough permits to do so. If it does not, it must buy additional permits on the open market. If the polluter has more permits than it needs, then it may sell the surplus. (Some systems, including the national sulfur dioxide trading system, also allow the polluter to retain the unused permits for use in a future year. This is called *banking*.) Note that the polluter is free to revamp its production system such that less pollution is emitted per widget generated. This will allow it to produce more widgets with the same number of permits and perhaps allow it to sell unused permits to other polluters.

As with environmental taxes, the marginal cost of pollution reduction that each societal actor faces will determine how it will respond to a tradable pollution permit regime. If an actor faces a marginal pollution reduction cost in excess of the market price of permits, then it will simply buy permits and continue to pollute. On the other hand, if an actor's marginal pollution reduction costs are lower than the market price of permits, then we would expect it to reduce its pollution and sell off any excess permits at a profit. In effect, then, those with lower costs of pollution reduction should reduce their pollution output more than those with higher marginal costs. This means that, in theory, the cost of attaining a particular reduction in pollution (to the total cap imposed by the tradable permit system) should be less than the cost would be if each polluter were required to reduce its pollution by a set amount. For this reason, tradable pollution permit regimes are said to attain pollution reduction cost-effectively.[5]

Note that although a typical tradable pollution permit regime caps the total amount of pollutant that can be emitted in the region over the course of a year (or other relevant time period), it does not speak to what the distribution of those permits within the region will be. For global pollutants whose harm is the same regardless of the point of origin, this is irrelevant. For regional and local pollutants, however, trading in permits may lead to a concentration of the harm resulting from emission of the pollutant at a few locations. (Even if the problem already exists before advent of the tradable pollution permit regime, the trading may exacerbate the problem.) These locations are called *hot spots*. Hot spots often tend to be found in areas populated by poorer people and members of minority groups. As we shall discuss later in this chapter, hot spots are of great concern to advocates of *environmental justice*.

Tradable pollution permits have become increasingly popular in recent years. Such a system, implemented among gasoline refiners, was first used to phase out lead from gasoline. In 1990, the Clean Air Act was amended to establish the first truly national tradable pollution permit system: a trading system for sulfur dioxide emissions among electricity-generating power plants. This system is discussed in greater detail in Chapter 4.

Commentators often refer to effluent- and technology-based environmental regulation as *command-and-control regulation*. Command-and-control regulation is contrasted with *market-based regulation*, which includes tradable pollution permit regimes and environmental taxes. The thinking here is that effluent- and technology-based regulations are commands issued by central government authorities. They apply to all polluters, indiscriminately. Therefore they do not take into account, for example, which polluters have higher or lower marginal costs of pollution abatement. In contrast, market-based regulatory instruments are not blind commands. They allow individual actors the flexibility to decide the best way to comply with the regulatory scheme (for example, to pollute and pay taxes or not). This allows market-based regimes to achieve pollution reduction at the lowest possible cost, that is, to be cost-effective. This is an important consideration, because money saved in achieving a particular level of pollution abatement can be used for other purposes that society deems valuable. It can be used to achieve even more environmental protection!

Still, one must be careful not to fall entirely into the trap of viewing all environmental regulation as either command-and-control or market-based. In fact, regulation falls on a spectrum. Consider, for example, that effluent-based regulation affords societal actors considerably more flexibility than does another form of command-and-control regulation, technology-based restrictions. The former allows actors to comply with the regulatory scheme either by installing pollution-reducing technology or, for example, by changing raw materials (if that leads to pollution reduction). In contrast, technology mandates require that particular technology be installed, even if some other action may be more cost-effective.

Although a tradable pollution permit system may offer the promise of cost-effective pollution reduction, we should also factor in other *costs to government*, such as the enforcement costs. We shall discuss enforcement options and costs a bit later in this chapter.

A final type of environmental regulatory strategy we have yet to address is information-based regulation. Two types of regulation fall into this category. First, the government may require the regulated entity to disseminate information to the public. The regulated entity could be the federal, state, or local government or a private actor. The idea is that the information may prompt the regulated actor to change its ways, whether on its own or in response to public pressure. Information is also valuable for individual actors who may wish to change their behavior, for example, in order to avoid certain pollutants.

A second type of information-based regulation asks a government body that is called on to undertake an action or make a decision—whether primarily environmental in nature or not—to gather relevant information on the likely environmental impact of the action or decision. Although a pure information-based regulation does not require the government to base its decision on the environmental report so generated, the thinking is that perhaps the information may have a substantive impact—again, either on its own or because of public pressure. This is the model on which the National Environmental Policy Act (NEPA)—discussed in Chapter 7—is based.

ENVIRONMENTAL LAW AND FEDERALISM

Another policy issue that has proven to be important in the development of modern environmental law is the question of federalism: How can, and should, regulatory power be vested among the various levels of government (federal, state, and local)? Historically, most environmental regulation was handled at either the state (think of tort law) or local (think of land use regulation) level. One exception was transboundary pollution—that is, pollution that traveled across state boundaries—which was to some degree handled under federal common law.

Today, things are quite different. Land use regulation remains substantially a matter of local concern, and toxic tort litigation and nuisance litigation may still be brought under state law. The U.S. Congress, however, has enacted numerous federal environmental statutes. Congress has relied on the Commerce Clause as its constitutional source of power in enacting these statutes. As we shall see shortly, the Commerce Clause may impose some outer limits on how far Congress can reach in regulating environmental quality. Of greater interest to us right now is the fact that Congress has chosen *not* to vest authority for administering and enforcing the federal environmental statutes solely in the federal government. Rather, Congress has invoked *cooperative federalism*. We shall examine the contours of cooperative federalism under various federal environmental regulatory regimes shortly; they tend to differ from regime to regime. What is common, however, among cooperative federalism regimes is that Congress in some way has enlisted the help of the states in achieving regulation.

Leaving to the side what Congress has chosen to do, let us ask what forms federal environmental regulation could theoretically take. First, federal regulation could restrict itself solely to dealing with issues of transboundary pollution. Were this the case, then states would be free to regulate — or not to regulate — environmental quality within their own borders. Only if pollution crossed into another jurisdiction (or, equally, if depletion of a resource within one jurisdiction somehow affected the resource in another jurisdiction, as it might with endangered plants or animals, for example) would federal restrictions be triggered. This has the benefit of leaving states free to decide what level of environmental protection to enact within their own borders.

As we shall see, some federal environmental acts do have provisions that specifically guard against transboundary pollution. As we shall also see, however, the federal acts regulate far beyond this concern.

A second possibility is that the federal government may set a *federal floor* for environmental protection. That is, the federal government may set a level of environmental protection below which the states are not free to choose. The states remain free, however, to set levels of environmental protection *in excess of* the federal level — hence, the description of the federal government as having set a regulatory *floor*.

Why may it be appropriate for the federal government to set such a floor? The answer turns on another story of motivations and actions grounded in economics — the so-called race to the bottom. Under the paradigmatic race-to-the-bottom story, jurisdictions compete for businesses to locate within their borders. One of the bases on which businesses choose where to locate is the cost of doing business. And one of the costs of doing business is complying with applicable environmental regulations. One may expect, then, that states that wish to have businesses locate there may enact environmental regulatory regimes that are less stringent — and, therefore, less costly to comply with.

One response to this argument is that people within the state may prefer to have higher levels of environmental protection and let their elected officials know that. Still, such individuals may not carry the day. For one thing, businesses may be more successful at communicating their wishes to government officials than unorganized individuals.[6] For another, a state with a high unemployment rate may have a lot of individual citizens who value the prospect of employment more highly than environmental protection.

Assuming that states have to compete for businesses and are willing to do so, then it is possible that states will, in turn, *bid down* the level of environmental protection. This, then, is the race to the bottom of the regulatory scale. The setting of a federal floor is meant to curb this tendency. It sets a minimal federal level of environmental protection, while at the same time leaving states free to choose greater protection if they desire. As we shall see, federal environmental statutes such as the Clean Air Act and Clean Water Act include provisions that preserve states' freedom to regulate in excess of, but not below, the levels of federal regulation.

Third, the federal government could make a *unitary federal choice* for environmental protection. As opposed to a federal floor that preempts state regulation below the floor, a unitary federal choice preempts state law in its entirety.[7]

Why might we want the federal government to do this? Put another way, given our understanding of federal-floor-type regulation, what is the problem with leaving states free to regulate in excess of federal regulation? The answer here is once again grounded in economics. Let us say that ThelaCo manufactures widgets. The widgets contain a substance, Pollutant P, that some believe to be environmentally unsafe. On this basis, states regulate the amount of Pollutant P that each widget may contain. The problem for ThelaCo is that each state chooses a different amount of acceptable Pollutant P, and the less Pollutant P is in the widget, the more costly it is to manufacture.

This leaves ThelaCo with a couple of choices. It can manufacture widgets with different levels of Pollutant P for sale in different states. This may be a costly option, however: Indeed, it may require ThelaCo to configure multiple assembly lines or factories that, but for the different regulatory levels, would be unnecessary.

Another option is for ThelaCo simply to manufacture one kind of widget. Assuming it wishes to be able to sell widgets in all jurisdictions, however, that widget can only contain as much Pollutant P as the most restrictive state will authorize. Thus, although ThelaCo may save on production costs in terms of the number of assembly lines or factories, its production costs will increase by virtue of the reduced levels of Pollutant P it may include in all widgets. Note that under this option, consumers in all states will enjoy the level of environmental protection chosen by the most restrictive states. Although this may in some ways be a benefit, consider that consumers in other states have not chosen (through their government representatives) such great environmental protection. Indeed, perhaps they affirmatively prefer to have widgets that are less environmentally desirable but cheaper. Instead, they must pay a higher price for more environmentally friendly widgets that they do not desire. In this sense, consumers in these states are subsidizing consumers in the more restrictive states. Put another way, the restrictive states are *externalizing* some costs onto consumers in other states.

Under these circumstances, one may think the federal government justified in coming in and simply enacting a uniform federal environmental standard. This will save ThelaCo the headache and cost of complying with multiple states' varying environmental standards or, in the alternative, giving one state (the one with the most restrictive regulatory standard) the effective power to choose the level of protection for everyone.

As we shall see, the federal government has enacted unitary federal standards under the federal environmental laws. For example, pesticide regulation tends to be national. Another example is automobile emissions, in which federal law allows states to choose between only two possible regulatory levels.

Which of these various possible forms should federal environmental regulation take? That depends on your priorities and which problems concern you the most. If you trust state and local government a great deal in terms of priority setting and enforcement, then you may opt for federal intervention only with respect to transboundary issues. If you think the race to the bottom is a problem, or if you think that there is some level of environmental protection below which governments ought not to be allowed to stray, then you may prefer a federal floor. (Note that federal law could both police transboundary pollution and also set a federal floor for environmental protection across the board.) If, on the other hand, you are interested in making sure that national markets and commerce remain viable, then you may instead choose full preemptive federal regulation.[8]

24

ENVIRONMENTAL LAW AND THE ADMINISTRATIVE STATE

The question of whether to vest power to regulate the environment at the federal, state, or local level is an important structural question. Another important structural question is whether to vest regulatory power in the legislative branch or in an administrative agency — that is, whether to proceed by statute or regulation. One may argue that the legislature is likely to be more responsive to the populace. On the other hand, there are reasons not to be confident in the legislature in this regard. First, one may think that the legislature may be *too* responsive to the public's wishes. There may be some risks of which the public is all too aware and *overestimates* and other risks of which the public is only dimly aware and *underestimates*. For example, the public may be overly concerned about the presence of any arsenic in drinking water,[9] but not as concerned as it should be about the presence of radon gas in private homes. In such cases, we may prefer to have experts at an administrative agency make choices about which risks to regulate and how to regulate them.

Second, legislators may be more subject to lobbying from and capture by industry than regulators are. In that case, again, regulators may be better actors.

Third, even leaving these points to the side, understanding environmental problems and regulation generally involves a fair understanding of the science involved. With all due respect to legislators, they are generally not in the best position to understand this science. Indeed, it is often said that environmental statutes are especially prone to be drafted by aides. Once again, regulators may be better situated to draft environmental regulations.

At the same time, there are reasons to prefer legislatures to administrative agencies. First, administrative agencies are less accountable to the public, and (notwithstanding the point just

25

mentioned about having too much responsiveness to public opinion being potentially problematic) we generally think accountability is a good thing.

Second, it is easy to overstate the case for regulators being objective experts as compared to legislators being political actors. Administrators and regulators are people, too. Moreover, even an administrative agency lies within the government. Indeed, as discussed in Chapter 2, the head of the prime federal government agency charged with environmental regulation — EPA — is nominated by the President and subject to Senate confirmation.

As we shall see (in Chapter 2 and elsewhere in the discussions of the particular regulatory regimes), the system we have adopts elements of both these options: Congress enacts statutes but delegates authority to EPA both to elucidate the structure of the regimes through regulation and also to enforce the regimes. We now turn to the question of enforcement.

ENFORCEMENT IN ENVIRONMENTAL REGULATION

A final preliminary consideration is the question of enforcement. We have in some ways assumed up to this point that the government — whether it be the federal, state, or local government — simply enacts some environmental regulation, and all societal actors just fall into line and obey the law. Needless to say, things aren't that simple.

Let us begin with enforcement of environmental laws against polluters. (It may be surprising that there could be enforcement against anyone else, but let us hold off on that now.) Let us consider three aspects of enforcement: first, what has to be enforced; second, who should do the enforcing; and third, how should enforcement be accomplished.

First, then, what has to be enforced? This will vary with the nature of the environmental regulation. If the regulation seeks to limit the amount of a substance that is in a product, then somehow the levels of the substances within the product should be tested. If, on the other hand, the regulation limits the amount of pollutant emitted, then emissions need to be tested.

For concreteness, let us consider the various types of end-of-pipe regulation that we discussed earlier. Consider first a technology requirement. This, presumably, requires enforcement of the installation of the technology. Consider next an effluent requirement. This requires enforcement of the rate at which pollution is emitted. Now consider a pollution tax. Insofar as the amount of tax due varies with the amount of pollution emitted, the enforcer must be able to determine the total amount of pollution emissions. The same is true for a tradable pollution permit system: Enforcement must ensure that no one emits more pollutant than the amount authorized by the emissions permits that he or she holds. Indeed, as we shall discuss shortly, the national sulfur dioxide trading system requires the installation of *continuous emissions monitoring equipment* as a means of enforcement.

Let's turn now to who should do the enforcing. An obvious answer is the government. Which level of government, however? One's first answer may be that the government that promulgated the regulation should enforce it. Thus, the federal government should enforce federal environmental law, state government should enforce state environmental law, and local government should enforce local environmental law. This answer is a little too facile, however. After all, to the extent that federal, state, and local environmental regulations overlap, do we really want to pay inspectors from all three governments to go about enforcing? Also, under the notion of cooperative federalism discussed earlier, it may make sense for the federal government to enlist state governments to enforce federal environmental laws. And, indeed, we will see some of that under existing federal environmental regimes.

Besides the various levels of government, there are others whom we may want to have the power to enforce the environmental laws: private individuals who suffer from violations of the law and environmental interest groups. Of course, we may think it appropriate and fair for victims to be able to recover for their losses and to enjoin future harm. Notice, however, that such plaintiffs also serve a role as private enforcers or, as they are sometimes called, *private attorneys general*. Why might we want private actors to be able to effect enforcement? It may be that government resources are being devoted elsewhere. Enforcement is costly, after all.

Our last question is how enforcement should be accomplished. One answer is civil fines. Another is disgorgement of profits. Taking things a step further, one might consider criminal liability. This would allow for the imposition of criminal fines and even jail time. And federal environmental laws do allow for criminal liability. Note, however, that criminal defendants accused of environmental crimes are entitled to all the protections that any criminal defendant enjoys. This means that it may be far easier, and less costly, to enforce the environmental laws civilly rather than criminally.

Do you remember that we said we were holding off on speaking about another kind of enforcement besides enforcement against polluters? Let us turn to this other kind of enforcement now. It may be surprising, but environmental law may authorize enforcement not only against polluters, but also against the government agency responsible for administering the environmental laws — at the federal level, EPA. Obviously, this is a different kind of enforcement. It is an action to force EPA to administer and/or enforce the environmental laws. For example, one may challenge a regulation that EPA has promulgated. As we shall see, many environmental statutes do authorize such enforcement actions.

Who would bring such an enforcement action? (Needless to say, it can't be EPA.) It would be someone, presumably, who is dissatisfied with an action that EPA has taken. Challengers tend to fall into two groups. The first group consists of environmental interest organizations and environmentally minded individuals; they tend to assail EPA regulations as too lenient on industry. The second group consists of industrial organizations (that is, organizations that represent the interests of particular industries) and industry actors (for example, owners of factories); they tend to challenge EPA regulations on the ground that they are too stringent. In many cases, EPA faces challenges from actors in both groups. (Indeed, it is sometimes loosely said that unless EPA faces both a challenge from environmentalists that a regulation is too lenient and a challenge from industry that it is too stringent, EPA has not done its job right!)

It is important to note the possible downside of allowing private actors to bring enforcement actions against EPA. EPA has limited resources, and it may be better at deciding how best to allocate those resources than individual private actors. Put another way, although individual private actors may be correct that EPA is technically obligated to do something, we might prefer it if EPA officials could consider everything that EPA is obligated to do and — especially in light of limited congressional funding — create its own prioritization of those obligations.

ENVIRONMENTAL JUSTICE

Another issue that has become of growing concern to environmental policymakers, and society generally, is environmental justice. Environmental justice addresses the balance between the distribution of the costs of environmental harms against the benefits resulting from the activities of which the environmental harms are a byproduct. For example, the pollution emanating from a factory may have large adverse effects on people living near the facility, whereas the benefits resulting from the factory's operation — the product being produced, employment, tax benefits — may be distributed much more widely. Environmental justice advocates question whether this unequal distribution of benefits and costs is fair and appropriate.

A paradigmatic setting in which environmental justice objections would be raised is one in which pollution-generating facilities all locate in one area of town. As noted earlier in this chapter, areas in which the harms of pollution are concentrated are called *hot spots*. It is all too common for hot spots to be areas in which the income of residents is comparatively poorer. Hot-spot areas also tend to be populated by members of minority groups.

There are three broad explanations for the trend that tends to find pollution-generating facilities in poor and minority areas. One is that factory owners — and government officials involved in facility-siting decisions — intentionally place such facilities in minority and poor areas. This may be because of racial or economic discrimination. A less cynical explanation is that residents in such areas tend to have less influence over politicians and access to the media to voice complaints. Put another way, wealthier individuals and those not in minority groups may have more influence over siting decisions.

A second explanation is that factory owners prefer to site their facilities in areas where land values are lower. Such areas tend to be areas in which the residents (if there are any) simply tend, for reasons unrelated to pollution, to be poorer and members of minority groups.

A third explanation is that even if factories are not initially sited (whether intentionally or otherwise) in poor and minority areas, such areas tend to become areas in which poorer and minority residents live over time. Why would this be the case?

The explanation is given in terms of *market dynamics*.[10] The placement of a polluting facility in an area tends to depress local real estate values. That — along with the deleterious effects of the pollution itself — may persuade residents with the financial wherewithal to move to do so. The lower real estate prices may also attract those with less money to spend on real estate (whether as purchasers or renters). Someone with less money may be more willing to accept risks of pollution (which are often unseen and therefore valued less heavily than perhaps they ought to be) in return for lower housing costs. Over time, then, areas in which pollution-generating facilities are located may become areas dominated by poorer residents and, to the extent that members of minority groups tend to be less affluent, minority residents.

What can be done to address environmental justice concerns? Consider first the placement of government facilities (such as public garbage incineration plants). One route is a procedural one: to call for greater transparency in government decision making and more avenues by which constituents — especially those who have tended to enjoy less access to government decision makers — can convey objections and arguments to those who will make the siting decisions. A second route is more substantive: to impose limits on government siting decisions by examining where such facilities tend to be located. Here, an important question to consider is whether it matters if the siting decisions were grounded in intentional discrimination. As we shall discuss in Chapter 8, enforcement is far easier when the siting decisions can be shown to have been intentionally discriminatory. Another important question is whether enforcement should be restricted to the government itself (that is, self-enforcement) or whether private actors should have standing to bring enforcement actions. As we shall discuss shortly, private enforcement has not been well received in this area.

What about private siting decisions? One tack is to consider whether, in order to site a facility in a particular location, the private actor must seek some kind of governmental approval — for example, an environmental permit or a zoning variance. If so, one may be able to use that as a trigger to use limitations on governmental siting decisions similar to those described in the preceding paragraph. Another possibility — and presumably the only option if government approval is not required — is to impose restrictions on private siting decisions. As we shall discuss in Chapter 8, the former approach is by far the more successful one.

CHAPTER RECAP

What have we learned in this chapter? There are many reasons to be supportive of environmental protection. Some are human-centered; some are not. Some are economic; some are not.

There are also many ways to go about structuring laws designed to protect the environment. The government may mandate that polluters take certain actions, or it may try to harness market power to achieve these goals. Another question is exactly who should make the decisions as to how to regulate. Environmental law can issue at the federal, state, or local level. Beyond that, the relevant legislature can enact detailed laws, or it may choose to delegate authority to the executive branch.

The question of how to enforce the environmental laws is also an important one. Civil and criminal sanctions against violators of the law are a possibility. One can imagine enforcement being handled by the government, private citizens, or both. It is also possible to allow enforcement by private citizens of legal mandates and deadlines against the agency charged by the legislature with carrying out the law.

ENDNOTES

1. Some commentators prefer the moniker *benefit-cost analysis*, sometimes premised on the claim that such analyses in practice too often undervalue or overlook the benefits of regulation.

2. Some nuisance cases consider the interests of others. For example, in *Boomer v. Atlantic Cement Co.*, 257 N.E.2d 870 (N.Y. 1970), the New York Court of Appeals noted the numerous employees at a cement factory that the plaintiffs were seeking to have shut down.

3. *See infra* Chapter 9.

4. It is also possible, though not common, to regulate the inputs used by those who generate substances or products, in an effort to reduce the pollution generated as byproducts during those processes.

5. In fact, pollution tax regimes have the same feature.

6. Note, however, that environmental organizations can help convey constituents' wishes to government officials.

7. It is possible to retain state law to the extent that it mimics the level of environmental protection chosen by the federal government.

8. Note that, in theory, the federal government could set the standard but leave the states to enforce that standard. In some ways, cooperative federalism models under existing federal environmental regulatory regimes choose this tack.

9. Professor Cass Sunstein has suggested that this may be due in part to familiarity with arsenic as a poison as used in the 1944 movie *Arsenic and Old Lace*. *See* Cass R. Sunstein, *The Arithmetic of Arsenic*, 90 Geo. L.J. 2255, 2262 (2002).

10. *See, e.g.*, Vicki Been, *Locally Undesirable Land Uses in Minority Neighborhoods: Disproportionate Siting or Market Dynamics?*, 103 Yale L.J. 1383 (1994).

∼ 2 ∼

Environmental Regulation, Constitutional Law, and Administrative Law

E nvironmental law raises interesting questions that intersect with other areas of law, including the law of federal courts, corporations, property, and torts. No other areas of law are of greater importance to environmental law, however, than constitutional law and administrative law. In this chapter, we will address the basics of these two areas of federal law as they relate to environmental regulation.[1]

CONSTITUTIONAL LAW

Two areas of constitutional law play especially prominent roles in environmental regulation: the Commerce Clause and the scope of federal regulatory power, and the Supremacy Clause and federal preemption of state law. A third area, eminent domain and the Takings Clause, is also of great importance. We shall consider each of these in turn. We defer consideration of a fourth area, the constitutional doctrine of standing to bring causes of action in federal court, until Chapter 8.

Commerce Clause

As set up by the Constitution, the federal government is one of limited, enumerated powers. A law enacted by Congress must rest on a power enumerated in Article I of the Constitution. Congress today draws perhaps its broadest powers from the Commerce Clause. The Clause grants Congress the power to "regulate commerce . . . among the several states."[2] A federal statute whose enactment rests on the Commerce Clause is invalid to the extent that it purports to grant jurisdiction beyond that authorized by the Commerce Clause.

Since the late 1930s, the Supreme Court has interpreted the Commerce Clause to afford Congress wide berth to pass laws that affect interstate commerce, even indirectly. Some 60 years later, the Court signaled a slight retreat from the broad interpretation given the Commerce Clause since the New Deal. In two cases, the Court struck down two statutes as lying beyond Congress's Commerce Clause powers.[3] Those cases, however, today remain exceptions; Congress's Commerce Clause power continues to enjoy broad scope.

The federal environmental statutes rest on the Commerce Clause. Might Congress have exceeded its Commerce Clause powers in enacting certain aspects of some environmental laws? The Supreme Court has at least alluded to this possibility in the context of the Clean Water Act. As discussed in greater detail in Chapter 3, Congress in the Clean Water Act extended federal power over "waters of the United States." The Court in *Solid Waste Agency of Northern Cook County v. U.S. Army Corps of Engineers*[4] invalidated a government regulation that interpreted the Clean Water Act to include federal jurisdiction over seasonal pools of water that lacked any connection at all to navigable waters. The Court indicated that if Congress were to have extended jurisdiction over such pools, it would be close to — if not beyond — its Commerce Clause limits. Relying on the canon of statutory construction that statutes should be interpreted to avoid unnecessary constitutional questions, the Court concluded that it should interpret the Clean Water Act not to extend to such pools and accordingly invalidated the government regulation.

The Supreme Court has not considered the constitutionality of the scope of other federal environmental statutes. Lower federal courts, however, have considered and rejected Commerce Clause challenges to the Endangered Species Act[5] and CERCLA.[6]

Dormant Commerce Clause

The preceding discussion illuminated the extent to which the Commerce Clause authorizes Congress to enact federal legislation and limits on that authority. The Commerce Clause has been interpreted to relate as well to state legislative power. Although state legislatures need not ground their enactments in the Commerce Clause or other federal constitutional provisions, the federal Commerce Clause has been interpreted by the courts to impose outer limits on state legislative authority (absent congressional authorization so to legislate). The limitation spawned by this jurisprudence is said to be based on the "dormant Commerce Clause."

The dormant Commerce Clause restricts a state's freedom to enact laws that either discriminate intentionally against out-of-state interests or impose more than an incidental burden on interstate (or international) commerce.[7] In examining the validity of a law under the dormant Commerce Clause, a court will give deference to state action that qualifies as an exercise of its police power to protect the health and welfare of its citizens.[8] A state is also given greater leeway to restrict interstate commerce in its role as a market participant, as opposed to its role as market regulator, to act in preference of in-state interests. Thus, state-run businesses have greater freedom to restrict out-of-state sales.[9]

How does dormant Commerce Clause jurisprudence relate to environmental regulation? It has arisen in cases challenging state authority to regulate the interstate market in garbage. As you may be aware, many municipalities ship their garbage out of the municipality, and sometimes out of state, for treatment and disposal. Recipient states sometimes balk at such arrangements and try to enact legislation to discourage or frustrate such trade. Courts have historically stricken such limitations under the dormant Commerce Clause. Most prominent among these cases is *Philadelphia v. New Jersey*, in which the Supreme Court invalidated a New Jersey ordinance that limited imports of waste from outside the state.[10]

On the flip side, consider the constitutionality of efforts to require local disposal of wastes. In 1994, the Court decided in *C & A Carbone, Inc. v. Town of Clarkstown*[11] that an ordinance forcing haulers to deliver waste to a particular private facility was invalid under the dormant Commerce Clause. Then, in its 2007 decision in *United Haulers Association v. Oneida-Herkimer Solid Waste Management Authority*,[12] the Supreme Court considered a challenge to a bi-county ordinance that required that solid waste and recyclables generated in the two counties be delivered to a county-owned waste processing facility. By a 5-4 vote, the Court upheld the ordinance. The Court distinguished *Carbone*, reasoning that because the processing facility at issue in *United Haulers* was publicly owned, the counties had validly decided to withdraw waste processing from the marketplace and therefore also from the purview of the dormant Commerce Clause.

Supremacy Clause

The Constitution's Supremacy Clause establishes that federal law is "the Supreme law of the land" and that it binds "Judges in every State . . . , any Thing in the Constitution or Laws of any State to the Contrary notwithstanding."[13] As a result, state law that conflicts with governing federal law is displaced because of what is called "preemption" of state law by federal law.

Courts have discerned three basic forms of preemption: *express preemption, conflict preemption,* and *field preemption.* Express preemption occurs where Congress explicitly states that state law is preempted.[14] Conflict preemption arises where, though Congress has not explicitly preempted state law, state law directly conflicts with federal law or clearly frustrates the goals of federal law. Field preemption occurs where, though the state law neither is expressly preempted nor directly conflicts with federal law, the statutory regime that Congress has enacted is seen as so complete and thorough that it displaces all state law, on the ground that Congress has chosen to "occupy the field."

Preemption arises under various federal environmental regimes. For example, Congress under the Clean Air Act vests authority to regulate motor vehicle tailpipe emissions with the federal government (although it preserves California's freedom to enact more stringent standards and then allows other states to elect to follow California standards) and expressly preempts state law that tries to do the same; the Federal Insecticide, Fungicide, and Rodenticide Act (FIFRA) preempts all inconsistent state law.

Preemption of state environmental law need not be complete. For example, as discussed in Chapters 3 and 4, the Clean Water and Clean Air Acts contain provisions that *explicitly* preserve states' freedom to enact laws that provide *more* environmental protection than does governing federal law.

Sometimes federal law is interpreted to preempt some, but not all, state law. Consider the question of whether a plaintiff in one state may sue a defendant in another state on a common law nuisance claim, in which the defendant argues that it has complied with governing federal law. As just noted (and discussed in greater detail in Chapters 3 and 4), the Clean Water and Air Acts preserve states' ability to apply standards more protective of environmental quality than federal law. On the other hand, to allow the defendant to face nuisance liability in two jurisdictions — its home jurisdiction and the jurisdiction of the plaintiff — may subject the defendant to two possibly inconsistent legal standards. The Court resolved this issue in the context of the Clean Water Act, holding, in the context of such interstate disputes, that the act leaves intact the common law of the source state but preempts the common law of the other state.[15] Accordingly, to return to our preceding paradigmatic example, the plaintiff can sue the defendant for common law nuisance, but only under the common law (though not necessarily the courts) of the defendant's state.[16]

As a final word, a limit on the power of the federal government vis-à-vis the state governments is worthy of note. Although the federal government is free to preempt state law and replace it with governing federal law, the federal government is not free to direct the state governments how to act. State governments remain free and autonomous governmental units. (Indeed, the Tenth Amendment instructs that "[t]he powers not delegated to the United States by the Constitution, nor prohibited by it to the States, are reserved to the States respectively, or to the people.") The federal government may, as it does under some environmental statutes, create financial incentives to entice states to enact certain laws or make certain decisions. It may not, however, "commandeer" the state governmental decision-making process.[17]

Eminent Domain and the Takings Clause

The Fifth Amendment to the U.S. Constitution guarantees "just compensation" whenever "private property" is "taken for public use." Implicit in this clause — known as the Takings Clause or the Just Compensation Clause — is the idea that the government can take property in the first place. This power is known as the power of eminent domain. The Takings Clause imposes a limit on the eminent domain power — that it be used "for the public use" — and also requires that just compensation be made when the power is exercised.

Though it was originally interpreted to apply only to the federal government, the Supreme Court has held that the Fourteenth Amendment renders the Takings Clause applicable to the states as well. Moreover, most state constitutions include an analogous provision.

The Takings Clause applies to physical occupations by the government, such as the paradigmatic setting in which the government uses its eminent domain power to acquire land to construct a roadway or public hospital. This has application to environmental regulation and protection: Consider the situation, for example, in which the government acquires privately held property for inclusion in a park.

Of at least as much, if not greater, importance to the setting of environmental protection is the applicability of the Takings Clause to another category of takings: so-called *regulatory takings*. A regulatory taking is a setting in which the government issues a regulation. The regulation does not divest the property owner of his or her interest in her property. It does, however, impose restrictions on his or her freedom to use the property.

Of course, many government regulations impose restrictions on one's ability to use one's property. Consider, for example, that a speed limit impinges on one's ability to drive legally in excess of the speed limit. The question becomes how to discern when a regulation is so restrictive that it qualifies as a regulatory taking that triggers application of the Takings Clause. As we shall see, this question has dogged courts over the years and continues to do so today. The question is of great importance for environmental regulations — such as historic preservation provisions and the Endangered Species Act, just to name two — that, though they leave ownership interests intact, impose limitations on property owners. Regulatory takings issues are also raised by application of section 404 of the Clean Water Act, which, by limiting deposits of dredged material, often effectively limits the development of property containing wetlands.

To begin, however, let us consider the stringency of the constitutional public use limitation on the eminent domain power. The Court recently affirmed that this limitation is not much of a limitation at all, at least from the perspective of judicial review of legislative determinations. In *Kelo v. City of New London*,[18] the Court considered the acceptability of the exercise of eminent domain power to take property from private homeowners and to give it in large amount to a private development. The "public use" justification offered by the government was, essentially, that the development project would increase tax revenues and improve the area as a whole. (Governments often use the eminent domain power to ameliorate "blighted" areas of town; there was no suggestion in this case that the area in question was blighted, however.)

The *Kelo* Court upheld the legislative determination that the exercise of eminent domain power was justified. In doing so, the Court held both that the definition of *public use* is capacious and that courts should defer to legislative determinations of what qualifies as a public use.

The *Kelo* case was one of those rarest of animals: a Supreme Court case that garners national media, and public, attention. The case generated a huge uproar. In response, legislation has been proposed (some enacted at the state level) that would curb the availability of the eminent domain power. This is entirely legal: Remember that the public use limitation is only a constitutional floor. State supreme courts are also free to interpret state constitutional analogs than the Supreme Court has interpreted the federal constitutional provision.

Because the federal constitutional public use limitation does not impose much of a restriction on exercises of eminent domain, the question becomes how to identify when the Takings Clause mandates compensation for government action. As discussed earlier, actual physical occupations (as occurred in *Kelo*) are clear: Compensation is owed. The larger question for our understanding of environmental regulation is when a *regulatory taking* occurs.

Regulatory takings date back to a Supreme Court case in the early twentieth century. The case involved a statute relevant to environmental protection: It prohibited coal mining that would allow subsidence of surface lands. The Court held that the statute constituted a regulatory taking. The opinion by Justice Holmes is not helpful in setting a clear legal standard, however, explaining only that regulatory takings occur when government action "goes too far."[19]

Recent case law has offered some clarification to the question of when a regulatory taking occurs, but not much. In *Penn Central Transportation Co. v. City of New York*,[20] the Court held that several factors should inform the inquiry: justice and fairness, the nature of the taking, the economic effect of the taking on the owner's reasonable investment-backed expectations, the diminution in value of the property that results from the taking, and the strength of the public interest.

Note that in determining the economic effect of the regulation in question and the resulting diminution in property value, the question of how one frames the property looms large. For example, *Penn Central* dealt with a New York City historical preservation provision that prohibited the owner of the Grand Central railroad station from erecting a skyscraper above the station. The owner argued that the percentage loss in value was 100 percent, because it lost the entire ability to use the air rights above the station. The Court, however, preferred to consider the air rights as only part of the entire property parcel: Because the owner continued to own the existing station, the loss of the right to use the air rights constituted a smaller percentage loss. Later Court cases have generally confirmed the position that one must look at the property as a whole in determining diminution in value.

What if a property owner takes possession of property after a government regulation that limits use of the property takes effect? Doesn't the existence of such a regulation on the books necessarily eliminate the property owner's "reasonable investment-backed expectations" that he or she could use the property in a way that the regulation prohibits? And, if so, wouldn't that preclude a takings claim? In *Palazzolo v. Rhode Island*, the Supreme Court held that such property owners are not barred from invoking the Takings Clause. Otherwise, the Court explained, the Takings Clause would have an "expiration date."[21] The case leaves open the question of whether, even if acquiring property after a limiting regulation has taken effect does not preclude a takings claim, it can be considered as a relevant factor. Concurring in *Palazzolo*, Justice O'Connor argued that it could, but Justice Scalia's concurring opinion specifically argued that it could not.

As we conclude our discussion of the Takings Clause, a couple of exceptional rules are worthy of note. First, what would otherwise be a taking will not be compensable if the effect of the regulation is simply to prevent the owner of the property from doing something with his or her property that would be a nuisance. The logic here is that, to the extent that the activity could be barred without compensation under a common law nuisance action, the Takings Clause ought not to compel compensation for causing discontinuation of the activity. Put another way, because state law defines property for Takings Clause purposes, one's property interest does not include the right to engage in activity that would be barred under a nuisance action.

Second, *Lucas v. South Carolina Coastal Council* announced a special rule for regulations that render the property in question practically devoid of value.[22] Such regulations need not be subjected to the *Penn Central* balancing test for their application to be considered a taking. Rather, the application of a regulation that renders a piece of property practically devoid of value is per se taking and automatically compensable, unless the activity barred would constitute a common law nuisance.[23]

Insofar as the *Lucas* standard provides a much easier path for a property owner to gain compensation as compared to the typical *Penn Central* balancing test, you may be wondering how close to zero the regulation at issue must render the property value in order to trigger the applicability of the *Lucas* per se test. Subsequent Court cases have revealed that the economic wipeout must be very close to 100 percent; a 93 percent reduction in value was not found sufficient to qualify for the *Lucas* test, for example.

ADMINISTRATIVE LAW

Let us begin our quick excursion through federal administrative law with an overview of the modern administrative state. Congress enacts statutes but, recognizing its limited expertise, delegates specific rule-making authority and enforcement to an administrative agency. In environmental law, the relevant administrative agency is most often the Environmental Protection Agency (EPA).[24] EPA is an independent federal agency. The head of EPA holds the title of *EPA Administrator*. The administrator is appointed by the President of the United States, with the advice and consent of the Senate.

45

Promulgating Regulations

When Congress enacts a statute and authorizes an administrative agency, such as EPA, to act under that statute, the administrative agency often issues regulations under the statute. The general procedures for doing this are set out under the federal Administrative Procedure Act (APA).[25] For our purposes, it suffices to note that EPA's goal is to develop a record of its rational rule making, for reasoned decision making, is what will protect the final regulation against court challenge. In general, the process is as follows. First, EPA decides what the relevant statute calls on it to do. It may perform scientific experiments, gather scientific evidence, and gather data from the industry to be regulated. After EPA decides initially how to proceed, it issues regulations in draft form; these are called *proposed regulations*. After that, EPA invites public comment on its proposed regulations. EPA then considers the comments it has received. EPA may choose to revise its proposed regulations in light of those comments. It may also choose not to. Either way, it explains publicly the reasons for its choices.

A final step in the regulatory process involves review by the White House Office of Management and Budget (OMB). Within that office, the Office of Information and Regulatory Affairs (OIRA) reviews regulations for compliance with executive orders, including in particular an assessment of whether the benefits of a regulation exceed its costs. Some presidential administrations have also afforded OMB and OIRA a virtual veto over promulgation of regulations. (Some assert that such a structure injects too much political control over the regulatory process.)

Once this review is complete, EPA publishes the regulations in final form. Only a court challenge can then delay their becoming effective.

What if an individual or an organization disagrees with EPA's final regulations? The APA authorizes such individuals or organizations to bring a court challenge. As noted earlier, challenges may originate with industrial actors who dislike the regulations because they are too stringent, or with environmental actors who dislike them because they are not stringent enough. In some cases, challenges may come from both sides.

Challenges may be based on different grounds. One common argument is that EPA has failed to gather adequate factual support and data to support its regulations. Where EPA has issued regulations under the typical notice-and-comment procedure, the APA directs that courts should uphold the EPA regulations generated unless they are "arbitrary and capricious." One important caveat here is that although EPA should be expected to gather evidence and address concerns that are reasonably within its purview, it need not reach out and address novel arguments that have not been brought before it. Accordingly, someone who wishes to challenge EPA is well advised to raise the argument during the rule-making administrative stage. To do so later may result in the court rejecting the argument as not timely raised.

Challengers sometimes assail, in particular, EPA's reliance on scientific evidence. When it comes to scientific evidence, however, courts tend to be deferential to EPA's choices of scientific experiments and scientific reasoning. The reason given is usually that EPA is an expert in the area, but courts are not. As one court put it: "[I]n reviewing EPA's actions here, this court does not sit as a scientific body, meticulously reviewing all data under a laboratory microscope."[26]

Finally, challengers sometimes argue that EPA's regulations are not consistent with the statute under which they are issued. The question arises, in other words, as to how much leeway the agency has in interpreting the statute. Here, one may think that challengers would often find relief in the courts. After all, although agencies are experts in many areas (such as science), if there is one thing in which courts are expert it is statutory interpretation. Yet in a famous administrative law case, *Chevron U.S.A. v. Natural Resources Defense Council*,[27] the Supreme Court came out the other way. Broadly speaking, the Court held that courts should defer to reasonable agency interpretations of statutes. Ever since, it is common to speak of agencies enjoying "*Chevron* deference."[28]

The Court in *Chevron* laid out the standard two-step test for *Chevron* deference.[29] In the first step — so-called *Chevron* Step One — the court should ask whether the statute as drafted by Congress is unambiguous. If it is, then EPA must interpret it according to its unambiguous meaning. If the statute is ambiguous, then the court should proceed to the second step — *Chevron* Step Two.

Under *Chevron* Step Two, the Court asks whether, in light of the ambiguity in the statute, EPA's interpretation is a reasonable one. If it is, then the court should defer to EPA's interpretation. Note that this means that a court may uphold an agency interpretation of a statute even if it is not the one that the court, left to its own devices, would have reached. Provided that EPA's interpretation is reasonable, the interpretation should be upheld under *Chevron*, even if another interpretation may also be reasonable.

So much for court evaluation of EPA regulations. What if EPA declines to act in the first place — that is, the challenge is to agency inaction, not action? Generally, the courts do not welcome challenges to agency inaction. Indeed, the APA calls for judicial review only of "final" agency actions.

Is this a problem? The answer is that it can be. Let's say that EPA drags its feet in issuing regulations. Note that such a scenario is quite possible. Recall, first, that EPA's administrator is a political appointee of the President and subject to Senate confirmation. Recall also (from Chapter 1) that we may expect administrative agencies to feel less accountable to the public and therefore freer not to fulfill congressional directives. Indeed, such scenarios did come to pass. In fact, in some ways, they were not surprising: Especially after the spate of environmental legislation enacted by Congress in the 1970s, EPA had a lot of demands on its plate, with limited time and resources to respond.

One actor that is well positioned to deal with EPA inaction is Congress. Congress can, and now often does, include timetables by which EPA is supposed to complete particular obligations. Then failure to comply with an applicable timetable may allow private actors to sue for noncompliance.

Also, if EPA is petitioned to engage in an action and rejects that petition, the rejection of the petition is a final action subject to review. One example of such a setting is found in the recent case of *Massachusetts v. EPA*. There, the Court considered an action by several jurisdictions and environmental organizations challenging EPA's rejection of a petition calling for it to regulate greenhouse gas emissions from motor vehicles under the Clean Air Act. The Court ruled against the EPA. The Court rejected both EPA's argument that it lacked authority under the Clean Air Act to regulate such emissions and also its argument that even if it did have authority, it validly exercised its discretion in choosing not to regulate. On the latter point, the Court examined EPA's proffered reasons for choosing not to regulate and found them disallowed as invalid under the clear statutory language.

Truly dilatory behavior on EPA's part may subject it to a suit for unreasonable delay even if a statutory deadline has not lapsed. Still, courts will be reluctant to find against an agency under such circumstances.

Other Agency Responsibilities: Administrative Adjudication and Enforcement

Agencies do not only promulgate regulations. They often also engage in adjudication and enforcement. On the adjudicative side, agencies sometimes resolve petitions for action and consider applications of regulations in particular settings. They also issue permits; permitting is seen as the application of law to a particular setting, and as such it falls within the purview of administrative adjudication. Some agencies also include judicial divisions that, through administrative law judges, hold "trials" over adverse proceedings between claimants arising under regulations.

On the enforcement side, agencies are often called on to enforce the laws and regulations for which they are responsible. We return to this subject in Chapter 8.

INTERPRETING STATUTES AND REGULATIONS

As we conclude this chapter, let us take a few moments to describe how we should read and conceive of environmental statutes and regulations in light of the discussion we have had of relevant points of constitutional and administrative law. To begin, a federal statute enacted under Congress's Commerce Clause (as most are) may not exceed the scope of the Commerce Clause. A regulation promulgated under a statute may not exceed the authorizing power of that statute (which, in turn, is bound by the Commerce Clause).

A regulation must be issued in accordance with the strictures of the APA and the relevant environmental statute. If the statute is clear, then the regulation must adhere to the plain meaning of the statute. If the statute is not clear, then a court will uphold the regulation — and the regulation is valid — provided that the regulatory interpretation of the statute is a reasonable one. Many federal environmental statutes include definition sections; these sections are relevant when one examines a regulation for consistency with a statute.

Let us turn now to state law. State law that is expressly preempted by a federal statute is invalid. So, too, are state laws that conflict with the goals of a federal statute, or state laws that try to regulate in an area in which Congress has sought to occupy the entire field. State laws are also invalid to the extent that they impose more than an incidental burden on interstate commerce, unless the state has a strong, nondiscriminatory purpose for the law. The state law may also survive the dormant Commerce Clause if the state is acting as a market participant, or perhaps if the state has chosen to act in the area to the exclusion of the market.

CHAPTER RECAP

What have we learned in this chapter? Constitutional law is hugely important to the implementation and application of environmental law. The Commerce Clause provides a basis for enactment of environmental laws. The dormant Commerce Clause precludes states from enacting restrictions on interstate trade even of polluting waste. The Supremacy Clause empowers the federal Congress to preempt state environmental laws. Last, although the Takings Clause recognizes government power to take and regulate property, it also requires government to compensate property owners for property that is taken and sometimes even for severe regulatory interference with property rights.

Administrative law is also of great import for environmental law. It provides the basis for the administrative state, which is the model for much of environmental law today. It provides guidelines for agencies — including EPA — to follow in promulgating regulations that implement congressional statutes. It also provides for judicial review of agency action.

ENDNOTES

1. It should go without saying that this chapter cannot offer even a thorough overview of all of federal constitutional law or federal administrative law. Instead, it will try to cover, in summary form, those points most important to understanding federal environmental law.

2. U.S. Const., art. I, §8, cl. 3.

3. *See United States v. Lopez*, 514 U.S. 549 (1995); *United States v. Morrison*, 529 U.S. 598 (2000).

4. 531 U.S. 159 (2001).

5. *See Nat'l Assn. of Home Builders v. Babbitt*, 130 F.3d 1041 (D.C. Cir. 1997); *GDF Realty Investments, Ltd. v. Norton*, 326 F.3d 622 (5th Cir. 2003).

6. *See United States v. Olin*, 107 F.3d 1506 (11th Cir. 1997).

7. *See Pike v. Bruce Church, Inc.*, 397 U.S. 137 (1970).

8. *See Maine v. Taylor*, 477 U.S. 131 (1986).

9. *See Reeves, Inc. v. Stake*, 447 U.S. 429 (1980).

10. 437 U.S. 617 (1978).

11. 511 U.S. 383 (1994).

12. 550 U.S. 330 (2007).

13. U.S. Const., art. VI, cl. 2.

14. An open question exists as to whether administrative agencies can preempt state law by explicit statements where Congress has not done so.

15. *See Int'l Paper Co. v. Ouellette*, 479 U.S. 481 (1987).

16. Even before the advent of the Clean Water Act, the Court had held that disputes between states over water pollution were governed by federal common law. *See, e.g., Illinois v. City of Milwaukee*, 406 U.S. 91 (1972). The Clean Water Act now governs these disputes. *See City of Milwaukee v. Illinois*, 451 U.S. 304 (1981).

17. *See New York v. United States*, 505 U.S. 144 (1992).

18. 545 U.S. 469 (2005).

19. *See Pennsylvania Coal Co. v. Mahon*, 260 U.S. 393, 415 (1922).

20. 438 U.S. 104 (1978).

21. 533 U.S. 606, 627 (2001).

22. 505 U.S. 1003 (1992).

23. Justice Scalia's opinion in *Lucas* indicates that the activity to be banned must have been considered a nuisance under "background principles of the State's law of property and nuisance." *Id.* at 1029. The precise scope of this assertion is open to debate.

24. As we shall see, sometimes the relevant agency is the Department of the Interior, the Department of Commerce, the National Marine Fisheries Service, or even the Department of the Army.

25. The Clean Air Act and the Endangered Species Act contain specific provisions that control regulatory action under some circumstances. *See* Clean Air Act §307(d), 42 U.S.C. §7607(d); Endangered Species Act §§4(h), 1533(h).

26. *NRDC v. U.S. EPA*, 16 F.3d 1395, 1401 (4th Cir. 1993).

27. 467 U.S. 837 (1984).

28. There are forms of agency deference other than *Chevron* deference. These lie beyond the scope of this brief overview.

29. Some commentators today speak of an additional step in the *Chevron* framework—so-called *Chevron* Step Zero—under which courts determine whether the setting is one in which the *Chevron* framework applies.

~ 3 ~

The Regulation of Air Pollution: The Clean Air Act

Many different chemical compounds can act as air pollutants.[1] Air pollutants include particulate matter suspended in the air and greenhouse gas emissions that rise to act as atmospheric insulation and lead to global warming.

Perhaps more than pollutants in other media, air pollutants can take the form of local, regional, or global pollutants. Heavier particulate matter may not travel far from its original emission point and thus may tend to have localized effects.

Sulfur and nitrogen oxides are precursors to acid precipitation. Acid precipitation (often taking the form of acid rain) falls from the atmosphere back to the earth. The resulting increase in acidity adversely affects bodies of water, including fish and other beings that live there, and also areas of land, where plant and animal life may be affected. Sulfur and nitrogen oxides may travel fair distances — sometimes hundreds of miles, for substantial distances across continents or oceans — before falling back to the earth. Thus, their effect is regional.

Greenhouse gases contribute to global warming. They have their deleterious effect once they rise in the atmosphere. The point of origin is irrelevant. In this sense, greenhouse gases are said to be global pollutants.

The primary tool through which Congress regulates air pollution is the Clean Air Act.[2] Congress created this act by amending previous statutes in 1970. As we shall see, it has been amended several times in the intervening years, as Congress has introduced new programs and shifted the balance of power between the federal and state governments. In general, the act is said to rely on cooperative federalism — that is, cooperation between the federal and state governments.

Congressional findings in the act's first section recognize the major air pollution problems that plagued the United States and to some degree continue to plague the country today.[3] Congress also set out the purposes it intended the act to fulfill. According to Congress, a "primary goal" was "to encourage or otherwise promote reasonable Federal, State, and local governmental actions, consistent with the provisions of [the act], for pollution prevention."[4] As we shall see, the act has not achieved much in the way of absolute pollution prevention. Among the act's other purposes are to "protect and enhance the quality of the Nation's air resources so as to promote the public health and welfare and the productive capacity of its population";[5] to "provide technical and financial assistance to State and local governments in connection with the development and execution of their air pollution prevention and control programs";[6] and to "encourage and assist the development and operation of regional air pollution prevention and control programs."[7] One can see here allusions to themes that are developed in the substantive provisions of the act: concern with public health and welfare, federalism, and regional air pollution control.

As we shall see, the act relies on health-based criteria to set air pollution levels. At the same time, the balancing of costs and benefits makes appearances (or at least has been interpreted to make appearances) in various provisions of the act.

In the end, the act emphasizes health, yet occasionally factors in costs and benefits. It also relies on considerable input from, and action by, individual states.

CATEGORIES OF SOURCES

At the outset, it is helpful to distinguish among different categories of sources — stationary sources, mobile sources, and indirect sources — the regulation of which are treated differently under the act. Regulation of stationary sources was largely left to the states under the Clean Air Act as enacted in 1970, subject to the proviso that states (as explained shortly) had to regulate internally in a way that achieves federally mandated ambient air quality standards. Subsequent amendments, however, have vested more and more direct federal requirements on these sources. Mobile sources — the most common of which are motor vehicles — are subject to direct federal regulation (although, as discussed shortly, California is statutorily authorized to regulate more stringently, with other states free to choose between the federal and California standards).

Finally, indirect sources are essentially land uses that, although they do not themselves result in any (or much) air pollution, attract activity that does result in air pollution. A paradigmatic example is a shopping mall. Although the mall itself surely directly emits some air pollutants, the real pollution concern one has with a mall is the pollution that results from the automobile traffic that the mall attracts. The act leaves indirect source regulation to the states.

NAAQS

The heart of the statute is found in the provisions governing the *national ambient air quality standards* (NAAQS). For pollutants for which NAAQS exist, the NAAQS provide the acceptable level of pollution in the ambient air. The NAAQS are national standards; they apply across the country. They are generated by the Environmental Protection Agency (EPA).[8]

For which air pollutants are there NAAQS? The act directs EPA to list each air pollutant whose emissions "may reasonably be anticipated to endanger public health or welfare."[9] For each such pollutant, EPA is further directed to issue "air quality criteria" that explain the pollutant's anticipated effects on public health and welfare.[10] These pollutants are accordingly referred to as *criteria pollutants*. At the time of the 1970 legislation, EPA had already issued criteria for sulfur dioxide, nitrogen oxides, carbon monoxide, and particulates. EPA is free to list additional criteria pollutants, and indeed the statute directs that it should. Nonetheless, in the years since, EPA has added only lead as a criteria pollutant — and that was only after a court ordered it to do so in response to a lawsuit by an environmental organization.[11] As this book goes to print, the identification of carbon dioxide as a criteria pollutant — which contributes to global warming — remains a possibility.

How is EPA to set the NAAQS for a criteria pollutant? The statute speaks of two levels of NAAQS — primary and secondary. Primary NAAQS are to be set at the level "requisite to protect the public health," with an "allow[ance] [for] an adequate margin of safety."[12] Secondary NAAQS call for a level "requisite to protect the public welfare from any known or anticipated adverse effects associated with the presence of such air pollutant in the ambient air."[13] Secondary NAAQS are promulgated to go beyond human health to protect other things that are important to humans, such as plant and animal life and human-made structures.[14] Therefore, they are (where they exist) at least as stringent as the primary NAAQS. In many cases, EPA has set secondary NAAQS at the same level as primary NAAQS or has not seen fit to promulgate them at all.

Note that although the NAAQS identify the acceptable level of pollution in the ambient atmosphere, they do not describe or prescribe the steps that should be taken to make sure that that level is achieved and maintained. Put another way, the NAAQS simply announce acceptable ambient pollutant levels; they do not put anyone on the hook for reducing pollution emissions. Still, they are important in that they set regulatory goals with which the states must endeavor to comply.

STATE IMPLEMENTATION PLANS

With particular exceptions described shortly,[15] the Clean Air Act leaves it to the states to decide how to achieve the NAAQS. The statute calls on each state to develop a *state implementation plan* (SIP).[16] The SIP must include (among other things) appropriate control measures and a timetable by which compliance with the NAAQS will be achieved. The state submits its SIP to EPA for approval.[17] The state retains freedom to allocate the burden of pollution reduction as it deems appropriate. So long as the SIP sets out a plan that is reasonably calculated to achieve NAAQS compliance, EPA may not reject the SIP. Thus, the Supreme Court rejected a utility's argument that EPA should have rejected the relevant SIP because compliance with the SIP would have been economically impossible for the utility.[18] According to the Court, the statute gives the state the freedom to decide how to apportion the regulatory burden. Thus, EPA cannot reject a SIP simply because it believes that the SIP will force some companies out of business or because EPA believes that another course of action would be preferable.

The statute expressly empowers the state to choose the regulatory tools that the SIP will employ. Among the tools the statute mentions as possibilities for inclusion in SIPs are "enforceable emission limitations and other control measures, means, or techniques (including economic incentives such as fees, marketable permits, and auctions of emissions rights), as well as schedules and timetables for compliance."[19]

SIP Calls

What remedy is available if EPA finds that a SIP submitted to it does not meet the minimal requirements called for by the statute or is in some way lacking? The statute authorizes EPA to call for revisions of the SIP in light of the deficiencies it identifies. This is called a *SIP call*. A state whose SIP is the subject of a SIP call will have the opportunity to revise its SIP to meet EPA's objections. Only upon failure to do so in a timely and satisfactory manner will EPA be free to impose its own remedy, in the form of a *federal implementation plan* (FIP). As is the case when promulgating a SIP, the state retains the freedom to decide how to comply with EPA's objections. It is not free, however, to dismiss EPA's objections. Most SIP calls have come in the wake of statutory or regulatory amendments (e.g., the issuance of a new NAAQS) or of a newly recognized air pollution issue (e.g., regional ozone problems).

Sanctions for Inadequate SIPs

If a state fails to submit a SIP or SIP plan revision (in response to a SIP call) or submits a SIP that inadequately provides for attainment of the NAAQS, the statute directs that sanctions be imposed.[20] These sanctions include a cutoff of federal highway funding[21] and more stringent federal regulation of the construction of new stationary sources in nonattainment areas.[22]

SPECIFIC FEDERAL PROGRAMS

As noted earlier, the states' discretion under SIPs is limited through particular federal programs that target specific air pollution problems. These programs apply only to *stationary sources*. The statute defines a stationary source as "any building, structure, facility, or installation which emits or may emit any air pollutant."[23] Some provisions apply specifically to *major stationary sources* or *major emitting facilities*; a source falls within the statutory definition if it "directly emits, or has the potential to emit, one hundred tons per year or more of any air pollutant (including any major emitting facility or source of fugitive emissions of any such pollutant, as determined by rule by the Administrator)."[24]

Requirements Based on the Area's Ambient Air Quality

As noted earlier, the states' discretion under SIPs is limited in some ways. One such limitation that Congress has imposed is to limit states' discretion in fashioning SIPs by imposing technology-based regulation of stationary sources, depending on the extent to which particular areas within a state are in compliance with the NAAQS.

Nonattainment

The act directs states to designate areas within their borders as either *attainment areas* (areas in compliance with the NAAQS) or *nonattainment areas* (areas not in compliance with the NAAQS).[25] Nonattainment areas have air quality worse than the NAAQS allow; accordingly, regulation in nonattainment areas is more stringent. The statute calls for implementation of all *reasonably available control measures* (RACM) — including, at a minimum, the installation of pollution reduction at a level consistent with the *reasonably available control technology* (RACT) at existing sources.[26] New and modified major stationary sources in nonattainment areas are required to meet a standard[27] defined as the *lowest achievable emission rate*

(LAER)[28] (in addition to the requirements of NSPS, discussed later). Further, a new source may pollute only to the extent that it obtains offsetting reductions from other sources in the region.[29]

Prevention of Significant Deterioration

Areas that are designated as in attainment are subject to the *prevention of significant deterioration* (PSD) program. The motivation underlying the PSD program is to reduce the likelihood that areas that are in attainment with the NAAQS will not fall into nonattainment. To the extent that the non-attainment program imposes strict limitations on new sources that locate in nonattainment areas, an incentive is created for new sources instead to locate in more pristine areas that are in attainment. Especially if a lot of sources are built in such areas, this may lead to severe deterioration of air quality. The PSD program seeks to ameliorate this problem by imposing limitations on new sources in attainment areas.

The PSD program directs that all attainment areas be classified as Class I, Class II, or Class III. Class I areas are those that are most pristine, including national parks.[30] Class II are areas that the state wishes to keep not quite as pristine as Class I areas but still fairly pristine.[31] The final category is Class III areas.[32]

Existing sources in PSD areas are not generally subject to regulation under the PSD program. In contrast, new major emitting facilities in PSD areas must incorporate the *best available control technology* (BACT).[33] This standard is statutorily defined as "an emission limitation based on the maximum degree of reduction of each pollutant subject to regulation under this chapter emitted from or which results from any major emitting facility, which the permitting authority, on a case-by-case basis, taking into account energy, environmental, and economic impacts and other costs, determines is achievable for such facility through application of production processes and available methods, systems, and techniques, including fuel cleaning, clean fuels, or treatment or innovative fuel combustion techniques for control of each such pollutant."[34] Further, the rate of increase in pollutant emissions is capped—most strongly for Class I areas and least strongly for Class III areas.[35]

By regulation, EPA has interpreted the word *source* to allow operators of stationary sources to offset increased emissions from a new facility against reductions in air emissions from an existing outlet at the same facility. This interpretation is known as the *bubble program* because in effect it allows operators of facilities to erect, for purposes of calculating of air pollutant emissions, an artificial bubble over the entire source— that is, both the new source and the existing source. Treating the bubble as a single source allows the operator to assert that there has no been no increase in emissions, such that new source review is not triggered. This is the case even though, were the new source treated as a stand-alone source on its own, it would trigger new source review (discussed just below).

Is EPA's interpretation of the statute correct? If you recall our discussion of administrative law and the rule of the *Chevron* case, then you may realize perhaps the correct question is not whether EPA's interpretation is correct but rather whether EPA's interpretation is valid. In the famed *Chevron* case itself—the case that spawned the *Chevron* rule and modern administrative law (which we discussed in Chapter 2)—the Court upheld EPA's interpretation. First, the Court reasoned that the language of the statute itself was ambiguous. Second, that being the case EPA's interpretation was a reasonable interpretation of the statute.

New Source Review

Another way in which state discretion to attain the NAAQS is limited is through *new source review*. Although in 1970

Congress left regulation of existing sources to the discretion of states under SIPs, it specified that new stationary sources would be subject to regulation as specified under the Clean Air Act.[36] The commonly understood justification for subjecting new sources to more stringent regulation is that it is far more expensive to retrofit an existing source to comply with a new standard than it is to construct a new source using state-of-the-art technology.

The statute directs that new stationary sources employ a *standard of performance* (*new source standards of performance* [NSPS]) that "reflects the degree of emission limitation achievable through the application of the best system of emission reduction which (taking into account the cost of achieving such reduction and any nonair quality health and environmental impact and energy requirements) the Administrator determines has been adequately demonstrated."[37] The fact that the standard of performance must be "adequately demonstrated" means that it must be one that is currently employed by at least some sources; in this sense, the standard is not technology forcing.

You may think that the inclusion of new source standards will have a pernicious incentive: To the extent that new sources are subjected to more stringent standards, owners of existing sources may be disinclined to construct new sources. Even if a new source would be economically and environmentally preferable, the owner of an existing source may choose instead to revamp the existing source. To deal with this, Congress specified that "modification[s]" of existing sources were to be included in the definition of *new source*.[38] The statute defines *modification* as "any physical change in, or change in the method of operation of, a stationary source which increases the amount of any air pollutant emitted by such source or which results in the emission of any air pollutant not previously emitted."[39]

Still, from the beginning, EPA has interpreted the statutory definition of *modification* to exclude minor repairs and renovations. The logic here, similarly, was to avoid creating a disincentive against making basic repairs to existing sources (as might be the case if such repairs triggered new source review). Over time, EPA investigated whether a particular repair or renovation of a particular source constituted a modification that would trigger new source review on a case-by-case basis. In the 2000s, EPA announced regulations that would expand the scope of the repair-and-renovation exemption. The regulations were met with challenges; although some were invalidated, many were upheld. The net result is that more repairs and renovations may be undertaken without triggering new source review.[40] The state of these amendments to the regulations is in flux under the administration of President Obama.

As discussed in the preceding sections, Congress has incorporated the distinction between new sources and existing sources into programs applicable to areas designated as *attainment* and *prevention of significant deterioration* areas. These programs generally impose even more stringent limitations on new sources. The programs incorporate by reference the statutory definitions provided under the basic new source provision. Thus, the issues raised (for example, in terms of defining modifications that trigger new source review) are essentially analogous to those discussed here.

Hazardous Air Pollutants

Another area in which Congress has taken discretion out of the states' hands concerns stationary source emissions of hazardous air pollutants — known by the acronym *HAPs*. Originally, Congress left it to EPA to identify HAPs. Over time, however, when EPA failed to identify many HAPs, Congress responded by promulgating a list of HAPs, with EPA free to augment the list as appropriate.[41]

With respect to HAPs, Congress has directed that EPA generate emissions standards reflecting "the maximum degree of reduction in emissions . . . (including a prohibition on such emissions, where achievable)."[42] EPA is to take into account other factors as well, including the costs of regulation and energy requirements.

The standards are set by category of source. Their validity is determined by reference to a *floor*. The standards for existing sources must be at least as stringent as the regulatory floor for the category. And, in turn, standards for new sources must be at least as strict as, and may be more stringent than, those for existing sources.[43]

How, then, does EPA identify the floor — that is, the minimum permissible regulatory level for existing and new sources — for a given category of stationary sources? The statute directs that the floor be set by reference to the standard achieved by the better-performing existing sources in the category. For categories encompassing 30 or more sources, the floor is (meaning that the standards must be no less stringent [but can be more stringent] than) "the average emission limitation achieved by the best performing 12 percent of the existing sources (for which the Administrator has emissions information)";[44] for categories with fewer than 30 sources, the floor is "the average emission limitation achieved by the best performing 5 sources (for which the Administrator has or could reasonably obtain emissions information) in the category or subcategory for categories or subcategories with fewer than 30 sources."[45] Put in more simple (though less accurate) terms, the statute sets the floor by reference to the average performance of the best (i.e., least polluting) existing sources.

Sulfur Dioxide Emissions Trading

Congress has also crafted federal responses to particular air pollutants. The most important of these is sulfur dioxide. You may recall from earlier discussion that sulfur dioxide is a precursor to acid precipitation, which has long been a problem in the northeast United States and in Canada as well.

Frustrated with state progress on the problem, Congress in 1990 instituted a tradable pollution permit regime with respect to major coal-burning electricity-generating facilities — the primary source for sulfur dioxide emissions. The regime is a market-based program; that is, it relies on economic incentives to achieve pollution reduction.

The program creates so-called sulfur dioxide emission *allowances*. Each allowance authorizes its holder to emit one ton of sulfur dioxide in the course of a calendar year. Those covered by the program may legally emit sulfur dioxide only to the extent that they hold permits sufficient to do so. If they lack sufficient permits, they may purchase additional permits on the open market. Alternatively, they must reduce their sulfur dioxide emissions. If they have more permits than they need, then they may sell the excess permits. Alternatively, one may hold unused permits for use in a future year; this is called *banking*. The total number of permits issued each year is less than the total tonnage of sulfur dioxide emissions in 1990. In other words, at 1990 levels, there are, colloquially, not enough permits to go around.

The initial phase of the sulfur dioxide trading program brought more than 200 of the largest electricity-generating facilities into the trading fold. Permits were initially allocated to existing facilities at no cost and in rough proportion to their prior polluting history.

The second phase, now in effect, has brought even more sources into the fold. Permits are allocated according to a formula, again at no cost, and again in rough proportion to each source's prior polluting history.

Note that even though electricity-generating facilities are covered by the sulfur dioxide trading program, it is legal for any entity, or even individuals, to purchase, hold, and sell sulfur dioxide allowances. Indeed, many environmental organizations have purchased allowances for the express purpose of "retiring" them and thus reducing the total amount of sulfur dioxide emissions.

Recall from Chapter 1 our discussion of tradable pollution permit regimes and the potential for creating or exacerbating "hot spots" of pollution effects. How does the national sulfur dioxide trading program avoid this concern? The answer is that essentially nothing in its design addresses the issue.[46] Fortunately, the available data indicate that trading to date has not created or exacerbated any hot spots.

REGULATION OF INTERSTATE POLLUTION TRANSPORT

If the Clean Air Act largely leaves it to the states to fashion SIPs designed to attain the NAAQS within their borders, how does the Clean Air Act deal with the problem of interstate air pollution transport? First, the Clean Air Act denies state authority to design a SIP based on the use of smokestacks that exceed what is called for by "good engineering practice."[47] The taller the smokestack, the farther in general the emissions from that smokestack will travel before falling closer to the earth's surface and affecting air quality. Thus, but for that provision, a state might simply call for the construction of very tall smokestacks, especially near borders with other jurisdictions. In that way, the state could try to preserve the quality of the air within its own borders, albeit while putting at risk the quality of the air in areas in other states across the border.

Second, the statutory provision that details the minimal requirements of a SIP mandates that each SIP include "adequate provisions . . . prohibiting . . . any source or other type of emissions activity within the State from emitting any air pollutant in amounts which will . . . contribute significantly to nonattainment in, or interfere with maintenance by, any other State with respect to any such national primary or secondary ambient air quality standard."[48] In other words, a state SIP must regulate in-state sources whose emissions interfere with NAAQS attainment in other states.

What happens if, nonetheless, a state believes that sources in another state are substantially contributing to nonattainment within the first state's borders? One answer is to hope — or to ask, though there is no formal legal authority so to demand — that EPA will issue a SIP call to review the offending state's SIP as inadequate. As with any SIP call, the state subject to the call will have the opportunity to revise its SIP to meet EPA's objections. Again, as is the case when promulgating a SIP, the state retains the freedom to decide how to comply with EPA's objections.

Another option — and one that provides legal relief — is provided by section 126(b) of the Clean Air Act. Section 126(b) empowers a state to formally petition the EPA Administrator "for a finding that any major source or group of stationary sources emits or would emit any air pollutant in violation of" the requirement that sources not substantially contribute to nonattainment in other states. The provision adds: "Within 60 days after receipt of any petition under this subsection and after public hearing, the Administrator shall make such a finding or deny the petition."[49] If the administrator rejects the state's petition or fails to render a finding within the statutory time period, then the petitioning state may seek judicial review. If the administrator ultimately grants the state's petition, EPA will regulate the offending sources directly. Note that unlike a SIP call, the state in which the offending sources are located is not legally a party to a section 126 petition; the state is not the object of the petition, nor is it the subject of any remedy (other than the loss of Clean Air Act regulatory power over the offending sources), nor is it free to determine how the offending sources will be regulated in order to ameliorate the section 126(b) violation. To date, most proceedings under section 126 have involved ozone nonattainment.

STATE FREEDOM TO REGULATE BEYOND THE CLEAN AIR ACT

We have been speaking about how many SIP requirements restrict state regulatory freedom to fashion SIPs. At the same time — except with respect to regulating automobile emissions where, as discussed shortly, Congress prefers to give states at most a choice between two levels of regulation — section 116 of the Clean Air Act preserves state regulatory power to enact laws not inconsistent with the Clean Air Act.[50] This includes the power to enact laws more protective of the environment than are the federal act provisions governing new sources and emissions of HAPs.

TITLE V PERMITTING

Permitting of pollution sources arose with the 1990 Clean Air Act Amendments, authority for which now resides in title V of the act.[51] Stationary sources subject to Clean Air Act regulation — and, in particular, major sources subject to the hazardous air pollutant, NSPS, PSD, and nonattainment programs — must seek permits. The permit explicitly restricts its recipient to pollute only as authorized under other provisions of the Clean Air Act;[52] it does not impose any independent pollution restrictions.[53] Its purpose is "to facilitate compliance . . . [by] consolidat[ing] all applicable requirements in a single document."[54] Title V contemplates state leadership in developing and administering permit programs.[55]

MOBILE SOURCES

One area over which states have never had discretion to regulate under their SIPs is emission of pollutants from mobile sources — that is, motor vehicles such as automobiles. The statute calls for EPA to regulate tailpipe emissions and also to require the use of more environmentally friendly fuels in areas of the nation with poor air quality.

Let us focus on the regulation of automobile tailpipe pollution emissions. The level of regulation varies with the model year of the vehicle. EPA has the power to introduce so-called technology-forcing regulations[56] — that is, standards for which there may not yet be existing technologies that will allow attainment of the relevant regulation. Regulations are announced in advance so as to give manufacturers time to develop appropriate technologies.[57]

For which tailpipe pollutants may, or must, EPA promulgate regulations? The statute directs the EPA Administrator to "prescribe . . . standards applicable to the emission of any air pollutant . . . which in his judgment cause, or contribute to, air pollution which may reasonably be anticipated to endanger public health or welfare."[58] In *Massachusetts v. EPA*[59] — a case raising the question of EPA's authority to regulate, and to decline to regulate, motor vehicle greenhouse gas emissions — the Supreme Court reviewed, among other things, the administrator's argument that the statutory phrasing "in his judgment" gave him absolute discretion to decline to regulate an air pollutant. The Court held that "EPA can avoid taking further action only if it determines that greenhouse gases do not contribute to climate change or if it provides some reasonable explanation as to why it cannot or will not exercise its discretion to determine whether they do."[60]

What about state authority to regulate automobile tailpipe emissions? Recall our previous discussion of section 116. That provision generally preserves state authority to impose regulatory requirements in excess of applicable federal standards. That provision, however, does not apply to the regulation of mobile sources. Indeed, to the contrary, the Clean Air Act preempts all state regulation inconsistent with federal regulation of tailpipe emissions.

That said, Congress did preserve a limited form of state autonomy. When the Clean Air Act was amended in 1970, California had already promulgated tailpipe emission standards as a result of poor air conditions in Los Angeles that prevailed even then. Congress in effect grandfathered California's authority to promulgate tailpipe emission standards. Specifically, California is free to seek an EPA waiver to set automobile emissions standards in excess of those required by EPA. Other states are then free to choose between EPA's standard and the California standard.

A separate statute, the Energy Policy and Conservation Act (EPCA), requires automobile manufacturers to make sure that their automobile fleets meet an average fuel economy, called a *corporate average fuel economy,* or CAFE (usually pronounced *café*).[61] CAFE standards are administered jointly between the secretary of transportation — who, through the National Highway Traffic Safety Administration (NHTSA) — sets the standards, and the EPA Administrator — who measures compliance.

Note that a lower CAFE standard translates into a higher number of miles a car can travel per gallon of gasoline, which in turn produces a reduction in emissions per mile traveled. Note also, however, that, while a lower CAFE standard will produce greater environmental protection, it may also increase the likelihood of serious injury and death resulting from motor vehicle accidents to the extent that manufacturers endeavor to increase fuel economy by producing lighter vehicles.

The statute has historically mandated a minimum CAFE for automobiles of 27.5 miles per gallon.[62] The statute authorizes the secretary of transportation to define other subcategories of motor vehicles and to set appropriate CAFE standards for them.[63] The higher CAFE standards applicable to light trucks enticed motor vehicle manufacturers to encourage consumers to purchase sport utility vehicles (SUVs), as opposed to automobiles; SUVs fall into the light truck category.

For many years, the automobile industry was able to stave off increases in the CAFE standard applicable to passenger automobiles. This changed with the enactment of the 2007 Energy Independence and Security Act,[64] which amended EPCA to require NHTSA to set CAFE standards for motor vehicle fleets — including both passenger cars and light trucks — such that fleets can attain a fuel economy level of 35 miles per gallon by 2020.[65]

The 2008 decision in *Center for Biological Diversity v. National Highway Traffic Safety Administration*[66] by the U.S. Court of Appeals for the Ninth Circuit is also noteworthy for its effect on CAFE standards. There, the court held that NHTSA was obligated to consider the effects global warming in fulfilling its obligations under the EPCA, and also under the National Environmental Policy Act (discussed in Chapter 7) with respect to setting CAFE standards.

THE CLEAN AIR ACT AND INTERNATIONAL LAW

Many air pollution problems extend internationally. We shall discuss two of these problems — ozone depletion and global warming — and international treaties designed to address them in Chapter 9. For now we note that Congress has enacted as part of the Clean Air Act statutory provisions designed to fulfill the country's obligations under the treaty regime addressing ozone depletion. We also note that the Clean Air Act includes a provision that empowers a foreign country to seek a SIP call to the extent that air pollution emissions from a state are substantially contributing to dangerous air pollution conditions in the foreign nation, but only if the foreign country gives the United States "essentially the same rights."[67] Finally, though the United States has yet to ratify the Kyoto Protocol — and thus to accept mandatory greenhouse gas emissions limits — EPA has recently announced that it plans to regulate domestic greenhouse gas emissions.

CHAPTER RECAP

What have we learned in this chapter? We have studied in some detail the structure of the Clean Air Act. The federal government issues NAAQS that set the goal for ambient air quality nationwide. States are then generally left to decide how the NAAQS can be achieved by regulating within their own borders. Congress has, however, introduced programs that restrict the discretion of states. New source provisions bring new pollution sources under direct federal regulatory standards. PSD and nonattainment programs subject areas that have acceptable, and even pristine, ambient air and poor air quality to federal regulatory standards. The cap-and-trade sulfur dioxide emissions trading program restricts the total annual sulfur dioxide emissions by electricity-generating facilities and provides for a free market in those emissions.

ENDNOTES

1. Some compounds may act as pollutants in some circumstances and offer health benefits in others. For example, at lower levels of the atmosphere, ozone is an air pollutant in that it is a chemical precursor to smog. In the upper atmosphere, by contrast, ozone acts as a shield against ultraviolet rays from the sun.
2. 42 U.S.C. §§7401–7671(q).
3. Clean Air Act §101(a), 42 U.S.C. §7401(a).
4. *Id.* §101(c), 42 U.S.C. §7401(c).
5. *Id.* §101(b)(1), 42 U.S.C. §7401(b)(1).
6. *Id.* §101(b)(3), 42 U.S.C. §7401(b)(3).
7. *Id.* §101(b)(4), 42 U.S.C. §7401(b)(4).

8. NAAQS thus differ from water quality standards under the Clean Water Act, which states are invited to promulgate for individual waterways, or even segments thereof. *See* Chapter 4.

9. Clean Air Act §108(a)(1)(A), 42 U.S.C. §7408(a)(1)(A).

10. *Id.* §108(a)(2), 42 U.S.C. §7408(a)(2).

11. *See Lead Indus. Assn. v. EPA*, 647 F.2d 1130 (D.C. Cir. 1980).

12. Clean Air Act §109(b)(1), 42 U.S.C. §7409(b)(1).

13. *Id.* §109(b)(2), 42 U.S.C. §7409(b)(2).

14. The Clean Air Act's definition section defines *effects on welfare* to include "effects on soils, water, crops, vegetation, man-made materials, animals, wildlife, weather, visibility, and climate, damage to and deterioration of property, and hazards to transportation, as well as effects on economic values and on personal comfort and well-being, whether caused by transformation, conversion, or combination with other air pollutants." Clean Air Act §302(h), 42 U.S.C. §7602(h).

15. These exceptions include newly constructed (and modified) sources, mobile sources, coal-powered electricity-generating facilities that emit sulfur dioxide, and mobile sources.

16. Clean Air Act §110(a)(1), 42 U.S.C. §7410(a)(1).

17. If a state fails to submit a SIP in timely fashion, the federal government will act in the state's absence by promulgating a federal implementation plan (FIP).

18. *See Union Elec. Co. v. EPA*, 427 U.S. 246 (1976).

19. Clean Air Act §110(a)(2)(A), 42 U.S.C. §7410(a)(2)(A).

20. *Id.* §179, 42 U.S.C. §7509.

21. *Id.* §179(b)(1), 42 U.S.C. §7509(b)(1).

22. *Id.* §179(b)(2), 42 U.S.C. §7509(b)(2). The general federal program for nonattainment areas is discussed shortly.

23. *Id.* §111(a)(3), 42 U.S.C. §7411(a)(3). The definition appears under the act's new source provision but is essentially incorporated by reference by other programs.

24. *Id.* §302(j), 42 U.S.C. §7602(j). The ozone nonattainment provisions include broader definitions of the term. *See, e.g., id.* §182(b)(1)(A)(ii)(I), 42 U.S.C. §7511a(b)(1)(A)(ii)(I). The prevention of significant deterioration program also contains a definition of *major emitting facility. See id.* §169(1), 42 U.S.C. §7479(1).

25. *Id.* §107(d)(1), 42 U.S.C. §7407(d)(1). Some areas may be designated as *nonclassifiable.*

26. *Id.* §172(c)(1), 42 U.S.C. §7502(c)(1).

27. *Id.* §172(c)(5), 42 U.S.C. §7502(c)(5).

28. This strict standard calls for "the most stringent emission limitation which is contained in the implementation plan of any State for such class or category of source, unless the owner or operator of the proposed source demonstrates that such limitations are not achievable, or the most stringent emission limitation which is achieved in practice by such class or category of source, whichever is more stringent." *Id.* §§171(3), 173(a)(2), 42 U.S.C. §§7501(3), 7503(a)(2). Note that the NSPS still is the minimum possible standard. *See id.*

29. Clean Air Act §173(c), 42 U.S.C. §7503(c).

30. *Id.* §162(a), 42 U.S.C. §7472(a).

31. *Id.* §162(b), 42 U.S.C. §7472(b).

32. *Id.* §164(a), 42 U.S.C. §7474(a).

33. *Id.* §165(a), 42 U.S.C. §7475(a).
34. *Id.* §§169(3), 165; 42 U.S.C. §§7479(3), 7475.
35. *Id.* §163(b), 42 U.S.C. §7473(b).
36. It appears that Congress's expectation was that eventually all sources that existed at that time would be taken offline so that all facilities would be subject to some direct federal regulation. That, however, has yet to happen, perhaps in part because of the incentives to which the grandfathering gives rise. For discussion, see Jonathan Remy Nash and Richard L. Revesz, *Grandfathering and Environmental Regulation: The Law and Economics of New Source Review*, 101 Nw. U. L. Rev. 1677 (2007).
37. Clean Air Act §111(a)(1), 42 U.S.C. §7411(a)(1). As discussed shortly, subsequent enactments have rendered this standard a floor, because higher standards may apply in both nonattainment and prevention of significant deterioration areas.
38. *Id.* §111(a)(2), 42 U.S.C. §7411(a)(2).
39. *Id.* §111(a)(4), 42 U.S.C. §7411(a)(4).
40. For discussion, see Nash and Revesz, *supra* note 36.
41. *See* Clean Air Act §112(b), 42 U.S.C. §7412(b).
42. *Id.* §112(d)(2), 42 U.S.C. §7412(d)(2).
43. *Id.* §112(d)(3), 42 U.S.C. §7412(d)(3).
44. *Id.* §112(d)(3)(A), 42 U.S.C. §7412(d)(3)(A).
45. *Id.* §112(d)(3)(B), 42 U.S.C. §7412(d)(3)(B).
46. The 1990 amendments allow EPA to explore the possibility of deposition standards "to protect sensitive and critically sensitive aquatic and terrestrial resources." Clean Air Act §401 note, 42 U.S.C. §7651 note. Also, the sulfur dioxide NAAQS remain in place and obligate states to take steps to attain them.
47. Clean Air Act §123(a)(1), 42 U.S.C. §7423(a)(1).
48. *Id.* §110(a)(2)(D)(i)(I), 42 U.S.C. §7410(a)(2)(D)(i)(I).
49. *Id.* §126(b), 42 U.S.C. §7426(b).
50. *Id.* §116, 42 U.S.C. §7416.
51. *See id.* §§501–507, 42 U.S.C. §§7661–7661f.
52. *See id.* §504, 42 U.S.C. §7661c.
53. *See N.Y. Pub. Interest Research Group v. Whitman*, 321 F.2d 316, 320 (2d Cir. 2003) ("Title V permits do not impose additional requirements on sources. . . .").
54. *See id.*
55. *See* Clean Air Act §502(d), 42 U.S.C. §7661a(d).
56. *See Int'l Harvester v. Ruckelshaus*, 478 F.2d 615 (D.C. Cir. 1973).
57. Clean Air Act §201(a)(1), (2), 42 U.S.C. §7521(a)(1), (2).
58. *Id.* §202(a), 42 U.S.C. §7521(a).
59. 549 U.S. 497 (2007).
60. *Id.* at 533.
61. *See* 49 U.S.C. §32902.
62. *See id.* §32902(b).
63. *See id.* §32902(a).
64. Pub. L. No. 110-140, 121 Stat. 1492.
65. *See* 49 U.S.C. §32902(b)(2)(A).
66. 538 F.3d 1172 (9th Cir. 2008).
67. Clean Air Act §115, 42 U.S.C. §7415.

~ 4 ~

The Regulation of Water Pollution: The Clean Water Act

L ike many other environmental statutes, the federal statutory scheme regulating water pollution was substantially amended in the early 1970s. The resultant regime
is called the Clean Water Act.[1]

Revision of the act and the concomitant strengthening of
federal regulation was a response to the growing recognition
that the nation's waterways were far from clean. Industrial pollutants had been dumped into rivers and lakes over the years,
and the ability of the waters to absorb high levels of pollution
was reaching its limit. You may recall, or have heard of, episodes
in which rivers caught fire. Needless to say, polluted waterways
pose threats to the health of individuals who draw drinking water
from them. It also poses health risks to people who swim, and
otherwise recreate, in them; it may also make water recreation
less enjoyable, even if only by virtue of a reduction in aesthetics.
Water pollution has adverse effects on beings who live in the
water, and then on people (and other animals) who feed on that
life. Polluted navigable waters can interfere with commerce to
the extent that waterways are relied on as conduits of goods.

Like the Clean Air Act, the Clean Water Act relies on cooperative federalism, and an active role for the states, in achieving its goals. However, the roles of the states and federal governments are quite different under the Clean Air and Clean Water Acts. In fact, one might say that they are almost reversed.

After canvassing the Clean Water Act, we briefly touch on another water-related statute at the end of the chapter. The Safe Drinking Water Act serves the important purpose of protecting the nation's sources of drinking water.

CLEAN WATER ACT

Goals

Water pollution is addressed under the federal law commonly known as the Clean Water Act. The act's opening section sets out several congressional goals, including "the national goal that the discharge of pollutants into the navigable waters be eliminated by 1985."[2] Such goals are laudable, but it is safe to say that most of them have yet to be met and may never be met. These goals (as with goals under other statutes) are still important. First, they are statements of aspiration that may inspire and signal the public about the importance of environmental values. Second, they may influence courts' interpretations of other, more substantive provisions of the statute.

The Federalism of the Clean Water Act: "Waters of the United States"

How broadly has Congress defined federal power to regulate water pollution? Recall that Congress has relied on the Constitution's Commerce Clause in enacting federal environmental statutes. Thus, it should come as no surprise that the

Clean Water Act at various points speaks of federal regulation over "navigable waters."[3] What is more surprising is that the Clean Water Act's definition section[4] includes a definition of the term *navigable waters*: "the waters of the United States."[5] Note that the definition does not include any reference to navigability.

More generally, what exactly does the phrase *waters of the United States* mean? In a trilogy of cases interpreting regulations purporting to define the scope of the phrase, the Supreme Court has shed light, though hardly clarity, on the relevant meaning.

First, in *United States v. Riverside Bayview Homes, Inc.*,[6] the Court upheld government regulation of wetlands. The wetlands in question were, of course, not themselves navigable but did abut a navigable waterway. In reaching its conclusion, the Court emphasized that Congress's use of the word *navigable* was of "limited import" by virtue of the expansive definition of *navigable waters* as "waters of the United States."[7]

In *Solid Waste Agency of Northern Cook County v. U.S. Army Corps of Engineers*,[8] the Court invalidated a government regulation that purported to define navigable waterways to include seasonal pools that did not in any way connect with any navigable waterways. Although recognizing that its opinion in *Bayview Homes* had described Congress's use of the word *navigable* in the statute as of "limited import," the Court emphasized that "it is one thing to give a word limited effect and quite another to give it no effect whatsoever."[9] The Court, however, did not pass on the constitutionality of the Clean Water Act. It simply applied a canon of statutory and regulatory construction that recommends interpretations that do not raise unnecessary constitutional questions to interpret the statute not to extend as broadly as the government had argued. It thus invalidated the government regulation as going beyond the scope of the statute.

Finally, in *Rapanos v. United States*,[10] a splintered Court rejected government regulation over wetlands that lacked a surface connection to a navigable waterway. A four-Justice plurality held such a connection necessary for federal jurisdiction as a matter of statutory interpretation. Four dissenting Justices would have upheld federal jurisdiction in the presence of a hydrological connection. Justice Kennedy, writing for himself, concurred in the judgment rejecting federal authority but seemed sympathetic to the standard enunciated by the dissent.

The decision has generated considerable confusion over the scope of the Clean Water Act. The plurality rule holds that there is no federal authority absent a surface connection to a navigable waterway. The dissent's view accepts federal authority on any connection — that is, not necessarily a surface connection — to navigable waters.

Lower courts have divided over how best to follow the fractured ruling in *Rapanos*. Some argue that insofar as Justice Kennedy's reasoning is similar to the dissent's, one should consider there to be five votes for the dissent's approach. On the other hand, traditional understandings — as enunciated by the Court itself — direct that where no opinion attracts a majority of Justices, the holding of the Court is to be determined on the narrowest ground agreed to by those voting in favor of the result garnering a majority of votes. Because those in dissent do not vote for the majority disposition, their reasoning plays no part in determining the Court's holding. On this understanding, then, only the plurality opinion and Justice Kennedy's concurrence determine what lower courts should do in the wake of *Rapanos*. Finally, some lower courts simply follow Justice Kennedy's swing-vote opinion. Congress may one day clarify matters through a statute; indeed, Chief Justice Roberts's dissent invited Congress to do just that.

Point Sources versus Nonpoint Sources

The Clean Water Act imposes the greatest burden on — and has been most effective with respect to — so-called *point sources.* Essentially, point sources are sources of water pollution that take the form of a readily identifiable point. Examples of point sources offered by the statute include "pipe, ditch, channel, tunnel, [and] conduit."[11] Importantly, the definition explicitly excludes "agricultural stormwater discharges and return flows from irrigated agriculture."[12]

Sources that are not point sources are so-called *nonpoint sources.* These sources produce water pollution discharges but not from a specific point of origin. People sometimes have trouble conceptualizing exactly what that may be. The most common class of nonpoint source pollution is agricultural runoff. To see why this is nonpoint source pollution, consider a farm in the wake of a storm. Rain from the storm may wash pollutants into an adjacent waterway (e.g., excrement from animals) that had theretofore lain undisturbed on the ground. There is no point source — no particular "point" whence the pollution originates — and so we refer to the pollution as nonpoint source pollution.

As we shall discuss shortly, nonpoint sources receive far less attention under the Clean Water Act. Why did Congress focus on point sources? There are three related reasons. First, insofar as point sources are easier to identify, their regulation is easier. Second, it is easier to attribute particular pollution to a particular point source than to nonpoint pollution sources. Third, when Congress enacted the modern Clean Water Act, the state of the nation's waters was pitiably bad; as mentioned earlier, some rivers even caught fire. Therefore, Congress focused on the sources of water pollution that were easiest and cheapest to regulate. Reductions in pollution from point sources were sure to make a difference in the quality of the nation's waters. And indeed they did. Today, by contrast, unlike at the time of the enactment of the modern Clean Water Act, most water pollution originates from nonpoint sources, and the comparatively minimal regulation of such sources poses a large problem.

Point Source Regulation and NPDES Permits

For now, let us focus on the Clean Water Act's regulation of point sources. Section 301(a) of the act includes a broad prohibition against "the discharge of any pollutant by any person."[13] At first blush, the language of the prohibition seems broad enough to encompass pollution from all sources (point or nonpoint), and indeed even pollution into media other than water (such as air pollution). The Clean Water Act's definition section, however, makes it clear that section 301's prohibition is limited to water pollution originating from point sources.

Even if it is limited to water pollution originating from point sources, the strong language of the section 301 prohibition remains promising; it seems to bar all such discharges. Notice, however, that the opening language of the subsection states that the prohibition is "[e]xcept as in compliance with" a variety of other Clean Water Act provisions. Thus, the section 301 bar is not absolute — in fact, far from it.

The most important exception to the section 301 prohibition is found in section 402. Section 402 is titled "National Pollutant Discharge Elimination System." This title also suggests that water pollution discharges will be eliminated, at least in the long term. In fact, however, we shall see that section 402 instead provides for a system of permits that *authorizes* water pollution discharges from point sources.

Any societal actor that discharges pollution from a point source into waters of the United States[14] should obtain a section 402 permit, otherwise known as an *NPDES permit*. Section 402 permits are issued either by the Environmental Protection Agency (EPA) itself or (as authorized under the statute) by a state environmental protection agency deputized by the federal EPA to act in its stead. Any deputized state agency must issue permits in the same way, and with the same content, as would EPA.

Effluent Limitations Under Section 402 Permits

A section 402 permit allows its holder to discharge pollution into water, but only if the holder complies with the permit's "effluent limitation" requirement. Generally speaking, an effluent limitation is a limit on the rate at which a polluting facility may discharge the pollutant in question. Effluent limitations are promulgated by EPA. They are set for categories of polluters. The stringency of a section 402 permit effluent limitation varies with two general factors: nationally applicable technology-based standards and, to the extent necessary, the water quality standards applicable to the body of water into which discharges of the pollutant are made. (We discuss water quality standards shortly.)

Although Congress has varied the stringency of the applicable effluent limitations over time, they have always been technology-based standards. As we discussed in Chapter 1, technology-based standards are not necessarily standards that require the installation of particular technology. The Clean Water Act effluent limitations fall into this category. Instead, the laws (and regulations thereunder) identify standards based on a particular type of technology (for example, the "best available technology economically feasible") for each class of polluter. They then determine a standard of pollution reduction that that technology can achieve and require all polluters in that class to attain that standard, whether by installing that technology or otherwise.

The statute draws a distinction among toxic pollutants, conventional pollutants (defined to include "pollutants classified as biological oxygen demanding, suspended solids, fecal coliform, and pH"[15]), and nonconventional pollutants (defined as pollutants that qualify neither as toxic nor conventional). The act effectively directs that the stringency of the applicable effluent limitations vary with the extent to which the pollutant poses a threat to the public health and welfare.

Congress has varied the stringency of technology-based standards over time. (We review the old standards both to give a historical perspective and also because some sources may still be grandfathered and operating under a standard less stringent than the one with which new sources would be required to comply.) Under the original 1972 act, all existing industrial sources of "non-toxic" pollutants were to meet discharge limitations reflecting the "best practicable control technology currently available," commonly called *BPT standards*,[16] and by 1983 these sources were to meet more stringent limitations reflecting the "best available technology economically achievable," commonly called *BAT standards*.[17]

In 1977, Congress divided nontoxic pollutants into two categories: *conventional* pollutants and *nonconventional* pollutants. It found that BAT would be unnecessarily costly for conventional pollutants and accordingly required polluters discharging such pollutants to be subject to the less stringent standard reflected by the "best conventional technology," or *BCT standards*.[18] Nonconventional pollutants remained subject to BAT, but the compliance deadlines for implementing BAT were extended.[19]

Congress originally let stand a health-based standard for toxic pollutants (including carcinogens) and directed EPA to identify and promulgate standards for such pollutants. This process was not successful; after five years, EPA had come up with proposed standards for only a few toxic pollutants and had finalized none. In 1977, Congress responded by amending the statute to incorporate a list of known toxic pollutants — generated by a consent decree — and directing EPA to come up with standards for those. Congress also mandated technology-based standards for toxic pollutants. Under the statute today, toxic pollutants draw the most stringent level of BAT effluent limitation.[20] EPA is directed, in promulgating these effluent limitations, to "take into account the toxicity of the pollutant, its persistence, degradability, the usual or potential presence of the affected organisms in any waters, [and] the importance of the affected organisms and the nature and extent of the effect of the toxic pollutant on such organisms."[21]

Before we proceed, let us pause to consider the varying stringency of the BAT and BCT effluent limitations, with a particular eye to the role that cost-benefit analysis plays in each. Among the factors EPA is to consider in establishing BAT is "the cost of achieving such effluent reduction."[22] Under BCT, in contrast, among the factors EPA is directed to consider are "the reasonableness of the relationship between the costs of attaining a reduction in effluents and the effluent reduction benefits derived."[23] BCT, then, unlike BAT, instructs EPA to consider the benefits derived from a more stringent standard, and also to consider whether those benefits bear some reasonable relationship to the costs the more stringent standard would impose. In this sense, we can see BAT to be more stringent than BCT.

Like the Clean Air Act, the Clean Water Act imposes more stringent requirements on new sources than it does on existing sources. A new source must comply with a "standard of performance." The "standard of performance" for new sources is statutorily defined as "a standard for the control of the discharge of pollutants which reflects the greatest degree of effluent reduction which the Administrator determines to be achievable through application of the best available demonstrated control technology, processes, operating methods, or other alternatives, including, where practicable, a standard permitting no discharge of pollutants,"[24] and is commonly referred to as *BACT (best available control technology) standards*. Unlike the other standards we have seen, EPA may not consider cost, and it may take into account possible changes in process — as opposed to technology — in developing the BACT standards.

Aside from variations according to the type of pollutant being discharged, the other general factor on which the stringency of a section 402 permit effluent limitation will turn is the industry type into which the permit holder's factory falls. EPA has long interpreted (with court approval) the Clean Water Act to allow it to establish applicable effluent limitations that vary with industry class.

You may be surprised that we have yet to mention how the quality of the water into which the pollution will be flowing affects the stringency of the effluent limitation imposed by a section 402 permit. After all, insofar as a section 402 permit allows for pollution from a point source to take place, one may think that the degree to which the permit requires pollution reduction measures may be affected by the cleanliness of the receiving waters. In fact, section 301 does allow for increasing the stringency of effluent limitations if necessary to allow the receiving water body to be in compliance with its governing water quality standards. (We discuss water quality standards under the Clean Water Act shortly.)

The generally applicable effluent limitations don't take individual polluter circumstances into account. What if a polluter contends that the otherwise applicable effluent limitation would be economically unworkable or poses a particular physical challenge? The statute (and the regulations thereunder) allows for section 402 applicants to seek a *variance* from the normal effluent requirements. These variances are available only under limited circumstances and are especially difficult to obtain for dischargers of toxic pollutants.

Nonpoint Sources

As noted earlier, the bulk of the Clean Water Act's regulatory zeal is directed at point sources. Are nonpoint sources regulated at all? The answer is, not much. Section 319 of the act directs that states should incorporate *best management practices* (BMP) in dealing with nonpoint sources.[25] This may mean, for example, having farmers plant certain trees and brush around the perimeter of their property to minimize runoff. The BMP standard is vague. More important, unlike the case of point sources, no permitting requirement or regulatory standard is imposed on individual non-point sources. Thus, enforcement of the best management practices requirement has proven illusive. The problem is left to the states to address under state management plans.

State Freedom to Regulate Beyond the Clean Water Act

Note that the Clean Water Act generally preserves state authority to enact laws more stringent than those called for by the Clean Water Act.[26] Thus, the federal act sets a regulatory floor, preempting only state laws that purport to offer less protection than does federal law.[27]

Water Quality Standards

We emphasize again that the regulation of point sources largely does not turn on the quality of water into which discharges are made. Clean Water Act regulation of nonpoint sources is weak and also does not turn on the quality of bodies of water receiving pollution discharges. How, if at all, then, does the Clean Water Act take water quality into account?

The answer is through a secondary mechanism known as *water quality standards*. Water quality standards are issued by the states. A water quality standard is issued for a body of water or for individual segments of a body of water.

A water quality standard consists of two components: the *designated use* and the *water quality criteria*. The designated use defines the use to which the water body (or segment thereof) is to be put. Designated uses include use as a public water supply, for recreation, for propagation of fish and wildlife, or for agricultural and industrial purposes. Regulations make clear that the ordinary minimally allowable use will protect fish and wildlife, although lower designations are also possible in some circumstances.

The second part of a water quality standard, water quality criteria, sets the maximum level of the relevant pollutant appropriate to accommodate the chosen designated use. In effect, the water quality criteria give a standard of ambient pollution against which the actual pollutant concentration can be measured.

Water quality criteria are most commonly expressed numerically; they can also be expressed via *narratives*. A narrative criterion simply calls for a quality of water that supports a particular use. For example, a narrative criterion may allow for "no toxic pollutants in toxic amounts." As another example, in one case, a court approved EPA's upholding state numerical criteria against a challenge that the criteria failed adequately to protect aquatic life on the ground that the numerical criteria would be read in conjunction with "separate narrative criteria protecting . . . aquatic life and wildlife."[28] Those numerical criteria, the court reasoned, "could require more stringent controls in some cases than would be required through use of" numerical criteria, to the extent that they represented "the human health criteria alone."[29] As these examples make clear, it is more difficult to verify compliance with narrative water quality criteria than with numerical water quality criteria.

Water quality standards must include an antidegradation provision. That is, if a water body is now meeting its designated uses, the state must include provision to protect that condition.

Notice that water quality standards simply set a standard for water cleanliness. That is, they set goals for pollutant levels in the ambient water. They do not impose limitations on any individual polluters or even on polluters as a class.

Indeed, water quality standards do not themselves set any limit on the amount of pollution that enters a water body, only on the effluent levels of pollution in the water body. As we shall see presently, another Clean Water Act regulatory mechanism — total maximum daily loads — does set limits on pollution input. Recall, however, from our previous discussion of section 402 permits, that section 301 allows for increasing the stringency of effluent limitations if necessary for the receiving water body to comply with its governing water quality standards.

Before we move on, let us pause briefly to compare the structure of the Clean Water Act with that of the Clean Air Act. Recall that the Clean Air Act calls on EPA to set the acceptable ambient levels of pollution (through the national ambient air quality standards) while generally leaving it to the states to decide how to obtain those pollution levels. In contrast, under the Clean Water Act, EPA promulgates national industrywide standards with which polluters must comply, whereas the states are empowered (subject to EPA approval) to define acceptable ambient pollution levels in water bodies within their borders.

TMDLs

The Clean Water Act directs that states promulgate *total maximum daily loads* (TMDLs) for water bodies (or segments thereof) for which the effluent limitations of NPDES permits issued for polluters who discharge pollution into the relevant water body are insufficient to allow attainment of the relevant water quality standards. The TMDL is the amount of the pollutant in question that can acceptably enter the water body on a daily basis,[30] while still allowing for attainment of the relevant water quality standard.

What effect does the promulgation of a TMDL have on existing polluters? Consider first point sources. Recall that the trigger for a state to issue a TMDL is that the effluent limitations in NPDES permits are insufficiently stringent to protect the water quality. In these circumstances, the act allows, as we mentioned earlier in our discussion of NPDES permits, for effluent limitations to be made more stringent than they otherwise would be.

What about nonpoint sources? Consistent with its general lax treatment of nonpoint sources, the Clean Water Act itself does not restrict nonpoint sources based on TMDLs. Note that this is often the crux of water quality problems, insofar as NPDES permits substantially limit pollution that originates from point sources. Indeed, a water quality standard is often unattainable even if no pollution emanated from any point sources, by virtue of severe nonpoint source pollution.[31]

Water Quality Standards and Interstate Considerations

Say that a river flows from one state into another. What if a polluter along the river in the upstream state applies for an NPDES permit whose issuance may affect the ability of a segment of a water body located in the other state to attain the relevant water quality standard? Must the first state (or if the first state's environmental protection agency has not been deputized to act under the Clean Water Act, then the federal EPA) take into account the downstream state's water quality standard?

The Supreme Court considered this question in the case of *Arkansas v. Oklahoma*.[32] There, EPA had decided that it was appropriate to consider the downstream state's water quality standard in determining the propriety and scope of the permit to be issued in the upstream state. The Court concluded that even if the statute was silent on the matter, EPA's interpretation was a reasonable one, and accordingly it upheld EPA's action.

The Clean Water Act and Foreign Disputes

The Clean Water Act authorizes the administrator to notify the source state of pollution that he or she "has reason to believe that pollution is occurring which endangers the health or welfare of persons in a foreign country, and the Secretary of State requests him [or her] to abate such pollution."[33] The statute also directs the administrator "promptly" to call a hearing to the extent that he or she believes that "such pollution is occurring in sufficient quantity to warrant such action, and if such foreign country has given the United States essentially the same rights with respect to the prevention and control of pollution occurring in that country as is given that country by this subsection."[34]

Section 401 Certification

Section 401 of the Clean Water Act affords states considerable power to issue water quality–related requirements over projects that require federal licensing. Specifically, the act requires state certification of any project that requires a federal license and that may result in a discharge into navigable waters within the state. Note that the provision requires only that the project in question may result in a "discharge," not necessarily the discharge of a pollutant; the Supreme Court has held that the discharge of water itself into the water body is enough to trigger section 401's applicability.[35] The Supreme Court has ruled that the requirements for state certification need not relate to, or address problems that result from, the discharge that serve as the trigger to allow the state to impose the certification in the first place.[36] Thus, the state certification may address water quality issues unrelated to whatever discharge into the water results from the project. Also, note that the statute allows states to impose conditions under which the project *may* result in a discharge; the fact that it ultimately does not is irrelevant.

Section 404 Permitting

By its terms, section 404 prohibits the discharge of dredged or fill materials into navigable waters without a permit.[37] The section 404 program is administered by the Army Corps of Engineers, with input from EPA; permits, called *dredge and fill permits*, are issued by the Army Corps.[38] Though section 404 generally applies to navigable waters, the program has focused on depositing dredged materials in wetlands, and more generally "filling in" wetlands.

Section 404 of the Clean Water Act is a device that is used to protect wetlands. Wetlands are areas that, for some portions of the year, are periodically inundated with water such that they can support vegetation typically adapted for saturated soil conditions. They include areas such as swamps, bogs, and marshes. Wetlands can form critical parts of hydrological systems: They support habitats for aquatic animals, they can filter excessive sediment and toxic pollutants out of adjacent waters, and, by absorbing water out of adjacent waters at times of high flow, they can reduce downstream flooding.

Note that the section 404 prohibition applies not to dredging itself, but rather to the discharge of dredged materials. Still, the act of dredging itself usually involves some fallback of material, even if in very small amounts. Can the corps use the virtual certainty of fallback as a trigger to regulate all dredging activity? The U.S. court of appeals for the District of Columbia Circuit has ruled that it cannot. In *National Mining Association v. U.S. Army Corps of Engineers*,[39] the court ruled that an attempt by the corps to do this would subvert section 404's focus on discharge of dredged and fill material, not dredging itself. The court ruled that the corps had jurisdiction only over fallback other than incidental fallback. The exemption for incidental fallback is now incorporated in the regulations.

In *Borden Ranch Partnership v. U.S. Army Corps of Engineers*,[40] the Ninth Circuit concluded that the corps had properly exerted jurisdiction over deep ripping operations. (Deep ripping occurs when large metal prongs are pulled across the wetlands base, tearing up soil, including the protective clay layer.) The Supreme Court heard an appeal in the case but divided evenly 4-4, thus leaving the Ninth Circuit decision to stand affirmed, with the Supreme Court's action having no precedential effect.[41]

The statute does not elaborate on the factors that the Army Corps should consider in deciding whether to grant a dredge and fill permit. Under regulations promulgated by EPA,[42] the person or entity seeking a permit must establish, among other things, that (1) there is no "practicable alternative" to the proposed activity that would have less of an impact, (2) all "appropriate and practicable" mitigation measures will be undertaken, and (3) the activity for which the permit is sought will not result in violation of any other federal or state law.[43]

The question of whether a practicable alternative exists has proven to be controversial and subject to some manipulation. For example, if one wants to build a luxury housing complex, there may be many possible sites, some of which will not involve affecting a wetland. On the other hand, if one wishes to build a community centered on boating, the inclusion of a dock necessitates building near water. Because construction projects can often be characterized so as to emphasize different features, the incentive for developers is to describe them so as to limit the possible number of practicable alternatives.

Section 404 permits are examined in light of the goal of "no net loss" of wetlands. This policy, widely endorsed by environmentalists, was advanced by George H. W. Bush as part of his first campaign for the presidency. The Clinton administration also embraced the notion, and many states have since endorsed it as well. The basic idea is that the total acreage of wetlands and, to the extent possible, the ecological contributions of wetlands should not decrease. The goal allows for the elimination of wetlands to the extent that (sometimes a daunting task) new wetlands can be created. *Mitigation banking* — under which wetlands are preserved or restored in exchange for the destruction of other wetlands — is a modern tool for implementing the "no net loss" goal.

SAFE DRINKING WATER ACT

The nation's water supplies are protected not under the Clean Water Act, but rather under the Safe Drinking Water Act (SDWA).[44] The act directs EPA to identify possible contaminants of water that, in its judgment, may have adverse effects on public health.[45] The contaminants so identified should be known or substantially likely to occur in public water systems.[46]

The SDWA employs a hybrid standard based on both health concerns and feasibility. For each contaminant it identifies, EPA is then directed to generate a *maximum contaminant level goal* (MCLG).[47] The MCLG for a pollutant is to be set at "the level at which no known or anticipated adverse effects on the health of persons occur and which allows an adequate margin of safety."[48] As the statutory language suggests, the MCLG standard is health based and does not consider cost. It is also precautionary.

The MCLG is not, however, the standard with which water suppliers need to comply. The statute requires EPA to generate standards based on the goals. Specifically, for each contaminant, a *maximum contaminant level* (MCL) is to be set "as close to the maximum contaminant level goal as is feasible."[49] The statute defines a standard as "feasible" to the extent that EPA concludes that there is a technology, treatment technique, or other means that works "under field conditions and not solely under laboratory conditions" and is "available (taking cost into consideration)."[50]

Thus, although it comes close to being a purely health-based, zero-risk statute, in the end the SDWA does not preclude the presence of contaminants — even those that may cause human health effects — in drinking water. Perhaps because this outcome is surprising and perhaps also because drinking water hits most people closer to home than any other environmental amenity, an agency conclusion that allows a contaminant in drinking water sometimes is met with displeasure and even anger. EPA's decision to set the allowable level of arsenic in drinking water is one such example.[51]

CHAPTER RECAP

What have we learned in this chapter? We have seen in some detail the structure of the Clean Water Act. The act's center is the NPDES permit system, which requires point sources of water pollution to obtain permits. These permits impose effluent standards on polluters. The permits may be issued by EPA or, in states that have environmental protection agencies deputized by EPA, by the relevant state agency. The effluent requirements, however, are generated by EPA.

Nonpoint sources are subject to far less stringent regulation. States are called on to have nonpoint sources implement best management practices. The total maximum daily load system may eventually provide an avenue to restrict nonpoint water polluters.

The section 404 program protects the nation's wetlands. A permit from the Army Corps of Engineers is required to deposit dredged materials, or fill materials, in wetlands.

The SDWA protects the nation's drinking water. It employs a hybrid standard that considers both health concerns and feasibility.

ENDNOTES

1. 42 U.S.C. §§1251–1387.
2. Clean Water Act §101(a)(1), 33 U.S.C. §1251(a).
3. *E.g., id.* §404(a), 33 U.S.C. §1344(a); *id.* §502(12), 33 U.S.C. §1362(12).
4. *See id.* §502, 33 U.S.C. §1362. As discussed in Chapter 2, most major federal environmental statutes include their own *definition sections*, that is, statutory provisions that provide definitions of relevant terms under each statute.
5. *Id.* §502(7), 33 U.S.C. §1362(7).
6. 474 U.S. 121 (1985).
7. *Id.* at 133.
8. 531 U.S. 159 (2001).
9. *Id.* at 171–172.
10. 547 U.S. 715 (2006).
11. Clean Water Act §502(14), 33 U.S.C. §1362(14).
12. *Id.*
13. *Id.* §301(a), 33 U.S.C. §1311(a).
14. We discussed earlier the definition of the statutory phrase *waters of the United States*.
15. Clean Water Act §304(a)(4), 33 U.S.C. §1314(a)(4).
16. *See id.* §301(b)(1)(A), 33 U.S.C. §1311(b)(1)(A).
17. *See id.* §301(b)(2)(A), 33 U.S.C. §1311(b)(2)(A).
18. *See id.* §§301(b)(2)(E), 304(b)(4); 33 U.S.C. §§1311(b)(2)(E), 1314(b)(4).
19. *See* Pub. L. No. 95-217, §56, 91 Stat. 1566 (1977) (amended 1987) (deadlines ranging from 1984 to 1987).
20. Clean Water Act §§301(b)(2)(D), 307(a)(2); 33 U.S.C. §§1311(b)(2)(D), 1317(a)(2).
21. *Id.* §307(a)(2), 42 U.S.C. §1317(a)(2).
22. *Id.* §304(b)(2)(B), 33 U.S.C. §1314(b)(2)(B).
23. *Id.* §304(b)(4)(B), 33 U.S.C. §1314(b)(4)(B).
24. *See id.* §306, 33 U.S.C. §1316.
25. *Id.* §319(a), 33 U.S.C. §1329(a).
26. *See id.* §510, 33 U.S.C. §1370.
27. The notion of federal floors is discussed in Chapter 1.
28. *NRDC v. U.S. EPA*, 16 F.3d 1395, 1405 (4th Cir. 1993).
29. *Id.*
30. A federal appeals court clarified that TMDLs must be expressed on a daily basis; a seasonal or annual load was unacceptable. *See Friends of the Earth, Inc. v. EPA*, 446 F.3d 140 (D.C. Cir. 2006).

31. *See Pronsolino v. Nastri*, 291 F.3d 1123 (9th Cir. 2002) (holding that TMDL had to be issued even where no point source contributed to pollution in the water body).

32. 503 U.S. 91 (1992).

33. Clean Water Act §310(a), 33 U.S.C. §1320(a).

34. *Id.*

35. *See S. D. Warren Co. v. Me. Bd. of Envtl. Protection*, 547 U.S. 370 (2006).

36. *See PUD No. 1 of Jefferson County v. Wash. Dep't of Ecology*, 511 U.S. 700 (1994).

37. Clean Water Act §404(a), 33 U.S.C. §1344(a).

38. Some states have limited authority to issue permits.

39. 145 F.3d 1399 (D.C. Cir. 1998).

40. 261 F.3d 810 (9th Cir. 2001).

41. *Borden Ranch Partnership v. U.S. Army Corps of Engineers*, 537 U.S. 99 (2002).

42. Both the Army Corps and EPA have promulgated regulations under section 404. The corps decides whether to issue permits based on consideration of the pertinent regulations.

43. 40 C.F.R. §230.10.

44. 42 U.S.C. §§300f to 300j-26.

45. *Id.* §300g-1(b)(1)(A).

46. *Id.*

47. *Id.*

48. *Id.* §300g-1(b)(4)(A).

49. *Id.* §300g-1(b)(4)(B).

50. *Id.* §300g-1(b)(4)(D); *see also id.* §300g-1(b)(4)(E), (5).

51. For discussion, *see* Cass R. Sunstein, *The Arithmetic of Arsenic*, 90 Geo. L.J. 2255 (2002).

～ 5 ～

The Regulation of Hazardous Wastes: RCRA and CERCLA

The generation, treatment, and disposal of hazardous wastes on and in land have proven to be a difficult challenge. Simply disposing of wastes in a landfill or in containers (or both) raises the possibility that, over time, the hazardous wastes may seep out. Moreover, what began as a threat to land may translate into a risk for other media. For example, hazardous waste that escapes a landfill may contaminate an underground water source, which may have ramifications for an entire watershed. (Indeed, this was the problem that arose at the famed Love Canal site in the late 1970s; Love Canal prompted Congress to enact the CERCLA statute.) An incineration facility that burns waste may also produce hazardous ash, as well as hazardous air pollution emissions.

Congress has responded to the problem of land-based hazardous wastes with two statutes: the Resource Conservation and Recovery Act (RCRA)[1] and the Comprehensive Environmental Response, Compensation, and Liability Act (CERCLA).[2] RCRA was enacted in the late 1970s and CERCLA in early 1980 in the waning days of the Carter administration. RCRA sets out guidelines for the generation, treatment, storage, and disposal of hazardous wastes. It has been described as a "cradle-to-grave" approach. CERCLA deals with situations in which hazardous substances escape from storage or disposal facilities, even years after they were placed there. Together, then, RCRA and CERCLA deal with hazardous wastes from cradle to grave, and beyond.

SOLID WASTE

Let us begin with RCRA and a basic question: What is hazardous waste? RCRA was enacted to be part of a larger preexisting statute: the Solid Waste Disposal Act (SWDA). RCRA defines hazardous waste as a subset of solid waste.

We should begin, then, with the definition of solid waste. The SWDA defines *solid waste* as "any garbage, refuse, sludge from a waste treatment plant, water supply treatment plant, or air pollution control facility and other discarded material, including solid, liquid, semisolid, or contained gaseous material resulting from industrial, commercial, mining, and agricultural operations, and from community activities." Note that, rather counterintuitively, the definition of *solid waste* extends to some liquid and gaseous materials. Apart from providing examples of what is a solid waste, the statutory definition also specifies some things that are not solid wastes. It expressly excludes from the definition "solid or dissolved material in domestic sewage, or solid or dissolved materials in irrigation return flows or industrial discharges which are point sources subject to permits" under the Clean Water Act.[3]

Note that the definition of *solid waste* emphasizes the fact that the substance is garbage, disposed of, discarded, a waste product. A substance that is in active use, then, cannot be a solid waste. As a corollary, then, it cannot be a hazardous waste. Presumably, too, a substance that is to be recycled cannot be a solid, or a hazardous, waste. Indeed, in *American*

Mining Congress v. EPA, the U.S. court of appeals for the District of Columbia Circuit agreed with the general proposition that materials destined for recycling as part of the industrial process that generated them were not solid waste.[4] The court reasoned that such materials had "not yet become part of the waste disposal problem."

What if a substance lies dormant for a period of weeks before it is used or recycled? A period of months? In a second *American Mining Congress* case, the District of Columbia Circuit held that only materials destined for "immediate" reuse in some ongoing project could avoid the classification of solid waste.[5] In practice, a 90-day period has been the benchmark to decide whether reuse is immediate.

HAZARDOUS WASTE

Something that is not a solid waste cannot be a hazardous waste. But not all solid wastes are hazardous wastes; rather, hazardous wastes are a proper subset of solid wastes. What makes a solid waste hazardous?

RCRA defines two categories of hazardous wastes: *listed* hazardous wastes and *characteristic* hazardous wastes. As the name suggests, listed wastes appear on a list of substances that the Environmental Protection Agency (EPA) has designated as hazardous. Thus, if one of those substances qualifies as a solid waste, then it is also a hazardous waste. It is possible to petition EPA to delist a hazardous waste, but the process is costly and a difficult one in which to prevail.

Characteristic hazardous wastes are solid wastes that qualify as hazardous by virtue of the fact that they exhibit one of four characteristics: ignitability, corrosivity, reactivity, or toxicity. Although EPA regulations provide technical definitions of these terms, essentially a substance is ignitable if it is prone to catch fire during routine transportation, storage, or disposal;

corrosive if it may tend to "eat away" at protective casing; reactive if it is at risk of engaging in chemical reactions with other substances, and toxic if it poses a risk to human health. Although one can easily check whether a solid waste is a listed hazardous waste simply by consulting the relevant list, it is more difficult to determine whether a solid waste exhibits one of the four key characteristics of characteristic hazardous waste. Waste generators bear the burden of making this determination and thus determining their obligation of RCRA compliance (subject, of course, to EPA monitoring and enforcement).

What if a hazardous waste is mixed with another substance or is treated in some way such that another substance is derived from it? Is the new substance that emerges also a hazardous waste?

The answer to this question depends on whether the original substance is hazardous by virtue of listing or characteristic. Under the so-called *mixture rule* — a regulation promulgated by EPA — a mixture of a characteristic hazardous waste with another substance is itself deemed to be hazardous; the same result holds, under the *derived-from rule* (another EPA regulation), for a substance derived from the treatment, storage, or disposal (for example, incineration) of a listed hazardous waste. In contrast, a mixture of a characteristic hazardous waste with another substance is hazardous only if the new substance exhibits the same characteristic that rendered the original substance hazardous or, equally, one of the other three characteristics. The same is true for a substance derived from a characteristic hazardous waste: Such a substance is hazardous only if it exhibits one or more of the relevant characteristics. Thus, it is far more difficult to use mixture and treatment methods to escape having a listed, than a characteristic, hazardous waste.

Note that RCRA specifically exempts pesticides from its coverage. As we discuss briefly below, pesticides are subject to regulation by the Federal Insecticide, Fungicide, and Rodenticide Act (FIRFA).[6]

RCRA — SUBSTANTIVE REQUIREMENTS

Now that we have established what exactly qualifies as a hazardous waste, we will examine exactly what restrictions RCRA imposes on those who create, transport, store, treat, and dispose of those wastes. RCRA was designed to provide cradle-to-grave tracking and regulation of hazardous wastes. Accordingly, the statute imposes requirements on three categories of actors: generators; transporters; and treatment, storage, and disposal facilities (known as TSDFs). As we shall see, the regulation of TSDFs is much more stringent than that of either generators or transporters.

Generators

Societal actors that generate wastes must determine whether they are hazardous (either listed or characteristic). Those that generate hazardous wastes must maintain appropriate records and ensure proper storage and labeling. They are also subject to periodic reporting requirements.

Transporters

Societal actors that transport hazardous wastes must comply with applicable restrictions issued by EPA and the U.S. Department of Transportation. Transported hazardous wastes must be packaged and labeled appropriately. Recordkeeping and reporting are also required.

TSDFs

TSDF operators must obtain permits to operate their facilities. They are subject to recordkeeping and security requirements, and personnel at the facility must be properly trained.

In addition, EPA regulations impose various technical standards, depending on the precise nature of the facility. These technical standards are designed to minimize the chance that hazardous wastes will migrate out of the facility and contaminate adjacent land and waters.

Finally, TSDFs are subject to financial requirements. These requirements are designed to ensure that moneys will be available over 30 years to cover plant closure and, if necessary, cleanup and mitigation.

Landfill Regulation

In 1984 amendments, the U.S. Congress, concerned over land and groundwater contamination, attempted to minimize the use of landfills. It required EPA to prohibit disposal of hazardous wastes in landfills unless it could be established that "there will be no migration of hazardous constituents" from the landfill. Congress included an exception for wastes that were treated so as to "substantially diminish the toxicity of the waste" or the risk that hazardous constituents would migrate. Taking the ban one step further, Congress directed that, in the absence of EPA regulations explaining when landfills might appropriately be used, their use was entirely banned.

In response, EPA moved to define treatment so as to give substance to the exception and avoid the absolute ban that otherwise would have arisen. EPA regulations offer a variety of landfill design alternatives.

CERCLA

As noted earlier, the CERCLA statutory regime — also sometimes called the *Superfund statute*, after the cleanup fund to which the statute gave rise — is structured to recoup costs incurred in cleaning up and mitigating releases of hazardous substances that take place after they have been placed in storage or disposed of. As we shall see, apart from setting up the Superfund, the statute establishes a liability regime. The liability regime in the original CERCLA statute was quite aggressive, following the suggestion of the "polluter pays" principle we discussed in Chapter 1. Later amendments to CERCLA have reduced the liability regime's stringency in the name of fairness and equity (with a nod to successful lobbying, of course).

Hazardous Substances

The CERCLA statute addresses releases of hazardous substances. The statute's definition section defines *hazardous substances* to include hazardous wastes as defined under RCRA, hazardous air pollutants as defined under the Clean Air Act, and toxic water pollutants as defined under the Clean Water Act.[7] The definition expressly excludes petroleum (which is covered by the Oil Pollution Spill Act) and natural gas. *Release* is defined as "any spilling, leaking, pumping, pouring, emitting, emptying, discharging, injecting, escaping, leaching, dumping, or disposing into the environment."[8] The statute often speaks of releases from a "facility," but *facility* is broadly defined to include, among other things, "any building, structure, installation, equipment, pipe or pipeline . . . , ditch, [or] landfill."[9]

Responses to Releases and Substantial Threats of Releases

CERCLA directs the U.S. President, acting through EPA, to assemble a list of sites that, by virtue of known or threatened releases of hazardous substances, are most seriously contaminated and most warrant cleanup.[10] This list is called the National Priorities List (NPL). It also authorizes the President, acting through EPA, to identify sites at which releases of hazardous substances, or substantial threats of such releases, may pose an imminent and substantial danger to the public health and welfare, and to respond accordingly.[11] The statute also creates a *Superfund* — that is, an account of moneys that are dedicated to financing federal cleanups of contaminated sites. The Superfund is financed by taxes on petroleum and certain chemicals and is augmented by moneys recovered under the CERCLA liability regime discussed shortly.

CERCLA authorizes two types of responses to the threat of a release of a hazardous substance: *removal actions* and *remediation actions*. Removal actions are quick fixes designed to ameliorate immediate threats. Remediation actions are larger undertakings designed to achieve a more lasting and complete cleanup of the site. CERCLA directs that cleanups be conducted so as "at a minimum" to "assure[] protection of human health and the environment" and to be "relevant and appropriate under the circumstances."[12] Cleanups must comply with any "applicable or relevant and appropriate" standards (ARARs) under federal law, as well as with state law requirements that are more stringent than federal law.[13]

CERCLA Liability

Overview

The heart of the CERCLA statute is its liability scheme. You may recall from the discussion in Chapter 1 of the "polluter pays" principle that CERCLA is the federal environmental statute that most closely conforms to that principle; indeed, the legislative history to the original CERCLA enactment in 1980 reflects strong congressional intent to make polluters pay. As we shall say, this intent is reflected in the statute's strong impositions of liability. At the same time, CERCLA liabilities can be large, and private actors often balked at being held liable, arguing either that they were not the actual polluters, or that the scope of liability was inequitable. As a result,

Congress has amended the statute over the years in efforts to make the liability scheme less draconian. These amendments have also sometimes reduced the resemblance of the statute to a true "polluter pays" regime.

Our discussion of CERCLA liability will proceed as follows. First, we will discuss the items for which one may be held liable under CERCLA (as well as one important category of costs for which CERCLA does not impose liability). As we shall see, CERCLA permits recovery of the costs of cleanup undertaken by the federal government and by a state government or private parties pursuant to CERCLA.[14] Second, we discuss the parties whom CERCLA puts "on the hook" for liability — so-called *potentially responsible parties* (PRPs). Third, we will turn to the nature of CERCLA liability. Finally, we will consider the limited defenses to CERCLA liability as well as particular exemptions and exceptions.

Scope

First, to the extent that the federal or state government has conducted a CERCLA removal or remediation action, the statute authorizes that government to recover its costs. Second, to the extent that a private party has conducted a cleanup, the statute allows it to recover "any other necessary costs of response."[15] Third, the statute permits governments to recover monetary damages for "injury to, destruction of, or loss of natural resources."[16]

You may notice that absent from these recoverable costs is one type of harm that one reasonably may expect to arise in the wake of the release of a hazardous substance: human mortality and illness. The omission is intentional.[17] Realize that CERCLA was drafted and enacted to respond to what was seen to be a gap in the law. State tort law already provided for, and still provides for, recovery for personal injuries. Accordingly, extending CERCLA liability was seen as unnecessary. However, CERCLA does affect the application of state statutes of limitations with respect to such actions: The statute directs that, for state law property and personal injury claims arising out of releases of hazardous substances from a facility, if state law "provides a commencement date which is earlier than the federally required commencement date" — defined as "the date the plaintiff knew (or reasonably should have known) that the personal injury or property damages . . . were caused or contributed to by the hazardous substance or pollutant or contaminant concerned"[18] — then "such period shall commence at the federally required commencement date in lieu of the date specified in such State statute."[19] Thus, the statute sets a uniform federal date on which statutes of limitations are to commence, but leaves in place applicable state law regarding the length of the limitations period.

Who Is Liable?

As described earlier, CERCLA describes broad classes of PRPs who may be liable for CERCLA costs. PRPs fall into six categories.

The first is the present owner of the facility from which the release originated. The second is the present operator of the facility. The owner and operator may be, but need not be, the same person or entity. For example, one person may both own and operate a facility; or, although a corporation may own the facility, an individual corporate officer may operate the facility.

When a corporation owns a facility, are the shareholders — or, in the case of a parent-subsidiary corporate relationship, is the parent corporation — potentially liable as a CERCLA owner? The Supreme Court considered this question in the case of *United States v. Bestfoods*[20] and concluded that the statute evinces no congressional intent to overrule the ordinary state law that the corporate veil shields corporate shareholders and parent corporations from personal liability. The Court did indicate, however, that ordinary rules of "piercing the corporate veil" may apply if the corporate form can be shown to have been a sham. The Court also indicated that just because share-holders or a parent corporation cannot be held liable as owners, that does not mean that they cannot be held liable as operators. Thus, for example, if a majority shareholder of a corporation effectively directs operation of the facility, then he or she may be held liable as an operator even if he or she cannot be held liable as an owner.

The third type of PRP is the owner of the relevant facility at the time that the release in question occurred. (Needless to say, this may be the same as the present owner.) Along similar lines, the fourth type of PRP is the operator at the time the release occurred.

The fifth category of PRPs consists of those who arranged for disposal or treatment — or who arranged for the transport for purposes of disposal or treatment — of hazardous substances. This class of PRPs — called *arrangers* and sometimes called *generators* — clearly includes individuals and entities that generate hazardous substances themselves and send those substances to treatment and disposal facilities. However, the legal standard for whether an actor is an arranger is perhaps the most challenging to apply. Consider, for example, a company, EllenCo, that owns raw material and contracts with another company, StanCo, to process the raw material into a finished product. As part of its production process, StanCo generates hazardous substances of which it disposes. Is EllenCo an arranger? A recent Supreme Court case clarifies that the critical element is the intent of EllenCo to have StanCo dispose of "at least a portion" of the hazardous substances.[21] Even after this decision, it seems that the various factors that courts considered in evaluating arranger status will remain relevant. One such factor is the extent to which EllenCo actually directs — or effectively has the power to direct — StanCo's production process, including its protocols for dealing with the hazardous substances. Another factor at which courts look is whether EllenCo retains title to the material in question; if it does, then EllenCo is more likely to be considered an arranger. Even if title is transferred to StanCo, many courts remain dubious and may still consider EllenCo an arranger if title is later transferred back to EllenCo, such that the transfer of title from EllenCo to StanCo and then back again is seen as a "sham transaction."

The last category of PRPs consists of *transporters* — that is, "any person who accepts or accepted any hazardous substances for transport to disposal or treatment facilities, incineration vessels or sites selected by such person."[22] Note that the concluding language introduces the requirement that a transporter have a role in "select[ing]" the destination for the hazardous substances. It has been held that a person or entity that transports a hazardous substance from one point to another on the same contiguously owned property still can qualify as a transporter.

The Nature of Liability

CERCLA liability has three important characteristics: It is strict, it is retroactive, and it is joint and several.

CERCLA liability is strict liability. It is not based on negligence. If you meet the description as a PRP, then you are liable. You can avoid liability only if you qualify for one of the limited defenses or exceptions or exemptions, discussed shortly.

CERCLA liability is retroactive. As suggested by the statutory inclusion of past owners and operators, it reaches back in time to hold parties liable. CERCLA retroactive liability has been held to extend back to activities that occurred even before the enactment of the statute.

CERCLA liability is joint and several. This means that any one PRP may be held "on the hook" for all relevant CERCLA costs. Any PRP or group of PRPs who are held liable are free to sue other PRPs for contribution. Note, however, that there is no guarantee that other PRPs will be subject to lawsuit or have any funds, especially if the other PRPs are corporations that owned facilities years ago and are now defunct. As we shall discuss shortly, some rules limit joint and several liability; they are not broadly applicable, however.

Defenses

There are only four defenses to CERCLA PRP liability. Because the fourth category consists of "any combination" of the first three categories, there really are only three basic defenses.

The statute makes clear that, to be available, the hazardous substance release must have resulted "solely" from the circumstances described in one of the defenses (or some combination thereof). The burden of proof lies with the PRP. If a PRP cannot establish entitlement to a defense by a preponderance of the evidence, then the defense is unavailable.[23]

The first two defenses are limited. Under the first, the release must result from an act of God, such as a storm or flood. Under the second, the release must be the result of an act of war.[24]

The third defense at first seems broad: "an act or omission of a third party other than an employee or agent of the defendant, or than one whose act or omission occurs in connection with a contractual relationship, existing directly or indirectly, with the defendant."[25] However, the provision goes on to require that the defense is available only when the PRP can establish by a preponderance of the evidence both that "he [or she] exercised due care with respect to the hazardous substance concerned, taking into consideration the characteristics of such hazardous substance, in light of all relevant facts and circumstances," and that "he [or she] took precautions against foreseeable acts or omissions of any such third party and the consequences that could foreseeably result from such acts or omissions."[26] The requirement of due diligence strongly limits the availability of the defense. Also, note that, the due diligence requirement notwithstanding, the defense is unavailable to the extent that there was a contractual relationship between the PRP and the third party that caused the release. Thus, for example, the defense is unavailable to an owner if a tenant caused the release, because the owner and the tenant had a contractual relationship.

Severability and Contributors of Small Amounts

Joint and several liability can be avoided if the PRP can show that its contributions of waste to a site are "divisible" from the waste contributed by others. The Supreme Court recently confirmed that the starting point for this analysis is the Restatement of Torts' provision on apportionment of harm.[27] However, making a showing of divisibility is not as easy as it may sound. First, it is not enough to show that a PRP's waste originated in a different place, or arrived at a different time, from other waste at the site. Rather, it must be shown that the waste that the PRP contributed did not escape and mix with other waste at the site. If it did, then divisibility will be unavailable. Second, bear in mind that the burden lies with the PRP to avoid joint and several liability. This means that there is a presumption that a PRP's wastes are not divisible from other waste at the site. Unless that presumption is overcome, joint and several liability applies.

Contributors of minimal amounts of hazardous substances to a waste site may be able to settle with EPA to avoid substantial liability. These settlements are called *de minimis settlements*. If EPA determines that a PRP contributed a de minimis amount of hazardous waste to the total amount of waste at a site, the statute empowers EPA to enter into an early settlement with that PRP that shields the PRP from future liability provided that the PRP is willing to pay a premium above what would otherwise be that PRP's equitable share.[28]

CERCLA further provides for a *de micromis exception* to CERCLA liability.[29] This exception requires a PRP to make two showings. First, the PRP must establish that it contributed less than 100 gallons of hazardous liquid waste, or less than 200 pounds of solid waste. Second, the PRP must show that its waste has not contributed significantly, and could not in the future contribute significantly, to the response action at the site. A similar exception is available for residential property owners and small-business and nonprofit owners and operators who have sent typical municipal solid waste to what is now a hazardous waste site.

CERCLA Exceptions: Lenders

Lenders, such as banks, often retain a security interest in property when they lend money to a property owner. This is common practice when banks extend a mortgage loan. If the owner winds up defaulting on the loan, then the bank may sometimes foreclose on the property. If that happens, the bank becomes the owner of the property until it can resell it.

As originally enacted, CERCLA threw a monkey wrench into this traditional arrangement: A bank that foreclosed on property and became a property "owner" ran the risk that it could become a PRP if the site in question became a hazardous waste site that required cleanup. CERCLA cleanup costs can be large, and banks had not included such costs in pricing mortgage loans. The risk of CERCLA liability thus threatened either (1) to reduce the availability of mortgage loans because banks would be less willing to issue them or (2) to raise the price of mortgages (in terms of interest rates, for example), thus effectively making mortgage loans less affordable and available. Still, lenders (and especially large banks) are well positioned to monitor the parties to whom they choose to lend money. Moreover, CERCLA's broad regulatory net suggests that lenders who foreclose are no more entitled to escape

CERCLA liability than anyone else. Indeed, larger banks that have substantial assets may be better able to weather a large CERCLA judgment against them than many other societal actors.

In the end, EPA saw the threat to the viability of mortgage markets as an unattractive scenario. The agency tried to mitigate the problem by providing guidelines that would shield lenders from CERCLA liability. Ultimately, Congress responded with a statutory fix.

The statute now provides a liability shield for lenders who foreclose, provided that they act in a "commercially reasonabl[e]" manner while they hold the property and that they dispose of the property in a "commercially reasonable" period of time. The bank must not "participate in the management" of the property. The phrase *participate in management*, however, is defined favorably to lenders not to include "merely having the capacity to influence" management.[30]

CERCLA Exceptions: Innocent Landowners

As originally drafted, CERCLA extended liability to all owners of hazardous waste sites, without regard to whether they purchased the site with knowledge of the underlying problem. Note that there is a logic to this approach: It creates a strong, societally beneficial incentive for would-be purchasers to conduct due diligence before actually purchasing any property. At the same time, due diligence does not always succeed at revealing underlying problems. In 1986, Congress amended CERCLA to provide a third-party *innocent landowner* defense. The burden of entitlement to the defense rests with the purchaser. The purchaser must show that he or she undertook "all appropriate inquiry" before purchasing the property and that he or she had no "actual or constructive knowledge" of the presence on the property of any hazardous substance.[31] A 2002 amendment has further clarified and elevated the extent of prepurchase due diligence required for the exemption to apply.[32]

The Future of CERCLA Sites and the Problem of Brownfields

What happens to a CERCLA site once it is cleaned up? Theoretically, the hazardous waste problem has been mitigated, but will new owners be willing to take a chance with the property? Note that CERCLA itself offers no guarantee that future liability will not arise if, for example, more of a hazardous substance is found to have been released. For these reasons, cleaned-up CERCLA sites sometimes sit vacant, and cleanups of contaminated sites stall. Governments have tried to develop tax and other incentives to spur investment in these so-called brownfields. Still, the problem remains a serious one.

OTHER FEDERAL REGULATION OF HAZARDOUS SUBSTANCES

Although detailed discussion lies beyond the scope of this book, it is appropriate to note the existence of two other federal statutes that regulate hazardous substances. FIFRA regulates the sale and use of pesticides. (Its existence helps explain the RCRA exemption for pesticides.) It requires manufacturers to conduct considerable toxicological testing before they can market new pesticides. It also regulates labeling of those products.

The Toxic Substances Control Act (TSCA)[33] regulates dangerous chemicals not covered by other statutes. Like FIFRA, it requires testing of new products, but the testing it requires is not as extensive as is required under FIFRA.

Finally, as discussed briefly in Chapter 7, the Emergency Planning and Community Right-to-Know Act of 1986 (EPCRA) requires companies to disclose to EPA when they have released toxic chemicals. From these reports, EPA assembles the *toxic release inventory*.

CHAPTER RECAP

What have we learned in this chapter? We have focused on RCRA's treatment of land-based disposal of hazardous wastes and CERCLA's liability scheme for cleanups necessitated by releases of hazardous substances.

To determine whether RCRA applies, one first must determine whether the substance in question is a solid waste. In not, then RCRA has no application. If so, then one must next determine whether the solid waste qualifies as a hazardous waste. A waste may so qualify if it either is listed as hazardous or exhibits certain characteristics. Substances derived from, or resulting from mixing a substance with, a hazardous waste may also be deemed hazardous.

Those who generate and transport hazardous wastes are subject to numerous administrative requirements. Those who treat, store, and dispose of these wastes are subject to even more requirements, including financial requirements meant to ensure that money will be available in the future to cover any cleanups that may become necessary.

CERCLA imposes a liability scheme on so-called potentially responsible parties (PRPs) who deal with hazardous substances when a release of hazardous substances occurs. Hazardous substances are defined to include substances defined as hazardous under other environmental statutes. PRPs include current owners and operators of the facility from which a release occurs; the owner and operator of the facility at the time the substances that now have escaped were stored or disposed of; transporters of the substances; and arrangers, that is, those who have arranged for the disposal or storage of the hazardous substances.

CERCLA liability extends to removal and remediation costs of cleaning up hazardous waste sites. The federal government may sue for recovery of its expenditures, as can a state government or private party if it has paid for a cleanup.

CERCLA liability is strict, retroactive, and joint and several. The available defenses are delineated in the statute and are narrow. Limited exceptions are offered for lenders who acquire real property by virtue of a security interest, those who contribute very small amounts of hazardous substances to a site from which a release has occurred, and innocent purchasers. Many of these exceptions generally require anyone seeking to invoke them to make some affirmative showings.

ENDNOTES

1. 42 U.S.C. §§6901–6992k.
2. *Id.* §§9601–9675.
3. SWDA §1004(27), 42 U.S.C. 6903(27).
4. 824 F.2d 1177 (D.C. Cir. 1987).
5. *American Mining Congress v. EPA*, 907 F.2d 1179 (1990).
6. 7 U.S.C. §§136–136y.
7. CERCLA §101(14), 42 U.S.C. §9601(14).
8. *Id.* §101(22), 42 U.S.C. §9601(22).
9. *Id.* §101(9), 42 U.S.C. §9601(9).
10. *Id.* §105, 42 U.S.C. §9605.
11. *Id.* §104, 42 U.S.C. §9604.
12. *Id.* §121(d), 42 U.S.C. §9621(d).
13. *See id.*
14. Cleanups are conducted against the backdrop of the *national contingency plan*, which EPA promulgates as a guideline to cleanup practices. *See id.* §105, 42 U.S.C. §9605. The statute allows for governments to recover costs incurred in undertaking a removal or remediation action "not inconsistent with the national contingency plan," *id.* §107(a)(4)(A), 42 U.S.C. §9607(a)(4)(A), and for others to recover costs incurred in undertaking a removal or remediation action "consistent with the national contingency plan," *id.* §107(a)(4)(B), 42 U.S.C. §9607(a)(4)(B). As the difference in language suggests, nongovernmental plaintiffs have the burden of showing that their cleanup actions were consistent with the national contingency plan.

15. *Id.* §107(a), 42 U.S.C. §9607(a). The definition section defines *response* as "remove, removal, remedy, and remedial action." CERCLA §101(25), 42 U.S.C. §9601(25).

16. *Id.* The statute defines *natural resources* to include "land, fish, wildlife, biota, air, water, ground water, [and] drinking water supplies." *Id.* §101(16), 42 U.S.C. §9601(16).

17. *See id.* §309(a)(2), 42 U.S.C. §9658(a)(2) (directing that state law shall apply).

18. *Id.* §309(b)(4)(A), 42 U.S.C. §9658(b)(4)(A). Special rules apply for "minor or incompetent" plaintiffs. *See id.* §309(b)(4)(B), 42 U.S.C. §9658(b)(4)(B).

19. *Id.* §309(a)(1), 42 U.S.C. §9658(a)(1).

20. 524 U.S. 51 (1998).

21. *Burlington N. & S.F. R. Co. v. United States*, 129 S. Ct. 1870, 1880 (2009).

22. CERCLA §107(a)(3), 42 U.S.C. §9607(a)(3).

23. *Id.* §107(b), 42 U.S.C. §9607(b).

24. *Id.* §107(b)(1), (2), 42 U.S.C. §9607(b)(1), (2).

25. *Id.* §107(b)(3), 42 U.S.C. §9607(b)(3).

26. *Id.*

27. *Burlington N. & S.F. R. Co. v. United States*, 129 S. Ct. 1870, 1881 (2009) (citing Restatement (Second) of Torts) §433(A).

28. CERCLA §122(g), 42 U.S.C. §9622(g).

29. *Id.* §107(o)(1), 42 U.S.C. §9607(o)(1).

30. *Id.* §101(20)(E), 42 U.S.C. §9601(20)(E).

31. *Id.* §101(35), 42 U.S.C. §9601(35).

32. *Id.* §§101(4), 107(r); 42 U.S.C. §§9601(40), 9607(r).

33. 15 U.S.C. §§2601–2695d.

~ 6 ~

The Protection of Endangered and Threatened Species: The Endangered Species Act

I n this chapter, we will discuss the congressional statute designed to protect species whose continued existence is endangered or threatened — the Endangered Species Act (ESA).[1] The ESA was enacted as part of the spate of environmental legislative enactments in the early 1970s. It was quite uncontroversial when it passed both Houses of Congress. Its implementation, however, has proven far more controversial.

ADMINISTRATION OF THE ESA

Unlike most environmental statutes, administration of the ESA does not rest with the Environmental Protection Agency (EPA). Rather, the statute divides responsibility between the Fish and Wildlife Service (FWS), which lies within the Department of the Interior, and the National Oceanic and Atmospheric Administration's National Marine Fisheries Service (NMFS), which lies within the Department of Commerce. The respective titles of these two services may suggest to you the division of labor that the U.S. Congress had in mind. The FWS bears responsibility for terrestrial, avian, and freshwater fish species, whereas NMFS is responsible for marine species and anadromous fish — such as salmon and sturgeon — that swim upstream to procreate. Note that insects that constitute a pest and whose protection would post an overwhelming and overriding risk to humankind are excluded from the act's coverage.[2]

LISTING SPECIES

The ESA provides protection for species that are listed as either *endangered* or *threatened*. A species becomes listed when the relevant government agency — either the FWS or NMFS — places it on the list of endangered or threatened species. The agency may make this decision on its own or private actors may petition the agency to do so, with judicial review available if it refuses.[3] The listing process is achieved through administrative rule making, under the procedures discussed in Chapter 2.

The statute provides guidelines for when an agency may list a species as endangered or threatened. A species qualifies as *endangered* under the act's definition if it is "in danger of extinction throughout all or a significant portion of its range."[4] A species is *threatened* if it is "likely to become an endangered species in the foreseeable future throughout all or a significant portion of its range."[5]

The statute identifies a number of factors that the FWS and NMFS should take into account in making listing decisions. These are (1) the present or threatened destruction or modification of the species' habitat or range, (2) overutilization of the species "for commercial, recreational, scientific, or educational purposes," (3) danger to the species posed by disease or predation, (4) the "inadequacy of existing regulatory mechanisms" to protect the species, and (5) other "natural or manmade factors" that affect the species' continued existence.[6] The statute further directs that the FWS and NMFS make all listing determinations based "solely on the basis of best scientific and commercial data available."[7]

Protection of a species may impose economic hardship on society and particularly on landowners whose property may constitute part of the species' habitat. May — or must — the FWS or NMFS take these and other economic considerations into account in deciding whether to list a species as endangered or threatened? The answer is no: Because the statute does not identify cost as a relevant factor, it may not be considered.

One question which you may be wondering about is what exactly constitutes a *species*? Readers with some background in science, particularly biology or ecology, know that the scope of the term is debated even among scientists. Even if you are not versed in the relevant science, you are probably aware that it is often possible to have interspecies breeding. In short, the correct definition of the term *species* is subject to debate.

It is no different in law. The definition found in the ESA is not really a definition at all. Rather, the act clarifies that *species* should be interpreted to "include any subspecies of any fish or wildlife or plants" as well as any "distinct population segment of any species of vertebrate fish or wildlife which interbreeds when mature."[8] The definition thus conveys a capacious understanding of *species*. As a result, courts defer to what the FWS or NMFS chooses to list as an endangered or threatened species.

CONTROVERSY OVER LISTING

Is the prospect for listing of a species as endangered or threatened likely to generate controversy? Environmental organizations generally lobby the FWS and NMFS to list species, and sometimes sue when they fail to do so. However, landowners and industry actors are often opposed to listing. To understand why, we must understand the restrictions that apply once a species is listed as endangered or threatened. We will turn to those restrictions in greater detail shortly, but for now it is enough to understand that the restrictions imposed are substantial. Once a species is listed, moreover, avoiding these restrictions is difficult. Accordingly, landowners and industry actors find it in their interest to fight the decision to list a species in the first place. As you read through the restrictions imposed by the ESA once a species is listed, keep in the back of your mind the importance of the original listing decision that brings these restrictions to bear.

DOWNLISTINGS AND DELISTINGS

Does the ESA permit species to be moved from list to list? Yes. Does it permit species to be removed from either list if the species is no longer endangered or threatened? The answer again is yes. You may have read recently that the bald eagle was *delisted*. One of the goals of the act is to restore endangered and threatened species to viability. If things go as planned, eventually all endangered species will be *downlisted* to the threatened list, and all threatened species should be delisted altogether. Of course, the road to recovery of endangered and threatened species is a rocky one. It is important, though sad, to note that a species will be delisted if it winds up going extinct.

DESIGNATION OF CRITICAL HABITAT

The statute directs that when an agency lists a species as endangered or threatened, it should also designate that species' *critical habitat*.[9] The statute qualifies this directive, however, explaining that the agency should only do so when it is "prudent and determinable."[10] The statute further authorizes agencies to incorporate cost considerations into the determination of whether to identify a species' critical habitat.[11] Put another way, although costs are irrelevant to the decision of whether to list a species as endangered or threatened, they are relevant when designating a listed species' critical habitat. The statute also directs that in determining the scope of a critical habitat, the agency should consider "the best scientific data available" and also the impacts of the designation on the economy and on national security.[12]

ESA RESTRICTIONS

Once a species is listed as endangered or threatened, many restrictions apply. ESA restrictions limit the actions of both the government and private actors. Many of these restrictions apply to both endangered and threatened species.

Restrictions on Federal Government Action: Consultation

Section 7 of the act requires all federal agencies to consult with the FWS or NMFS (as appropriate) for various purposes, including to "conserv[e]" endangered and threatened species,[13] and with respect to "any agency action which is likely to jeopardize the continued existence of any species proposed to be listed under [the act] or result in the destruction or adverse modification of critical habitat proposed to be designated for such species."[14] Perhaps section 7's most important consultation requirement is the requirement for a federal agency undertaking such actions (called an *action agency*) to consult with the FWS or NMFS (the so-called *expert agency*) to ensure that any government action is "not likely to jeopardize the continued existence" of any "endangered or threatened species" or to "result in the destruction or adverse modification" of the species' critical habitat.[15]

After revisions to the regulatory scheme by the Obama administration, the decision as to whether formal consultation is required falls to the so-called expert agency — that is, the FWS or NMFS. Formal consultation is required when (1) a listed species is present in the area where government action will occur and (2) the activity in question may adversely affect that species or its critical habitat.[16] In contrast, no formal consultation is required if, after a biological assessment[17] or informal consultation with the FWS or NMFS, the agency concludes — and the FWS or NMFS concurs — that the action in question will not adversely affect a listed species or critical habitat.[18]

If the government action may adversely affect a listed species or critical habitat, then a biological opinion must be prepared. That opinion will assess whether the action in question is likely to adversely affect the listed species or critical habitat. If that opinion indicates that adverse effects are unlikely, then again a formal consultation is unnecessary.[19]

If formal consultation is required, then the FWS or NMFS must (1) review all the information provided to it;[20] (2) "[e]valuate the current status of the listed species or critical habitat;"[21] (3) "[e]valuate the effects of the action and cumulative effects on the listed species or critical habitat;"[22] and (4) "[f]ormulate its biological opinion as to whether the action, taken together with cumulative effects, is likely to jeopardize the continued existence of listed species or result in the destruction or adverse modification of critical habitat"[23] (a *jeopardy opinion*) or not (a *no jeopardy opinion*). The FWS or NMFS will then discuss with the federal agency (and any applicant) its review and evaluation and the basis for the finding in the biological opinion.[24] If a jeopardy opinion is to be issued, the FWS or NMFS will also discuss the "availability of reasonable and prudent alternatives (if a jeopardy opinion is to be issued) that the agency and the applicant can take to avoid violation of section 7(a)(2)."[25]

The FWS or NMFS may issue a no jeopardy opinion on the ground that the action (or the implementation of any reasonable and prudent alternatives) will result only in "incidental take of listed species," and accordingly "will not violate section 7(a)(2)."[26] In that instance, the FWS or NMFS will "provide with the biological opinion a statement concerning incidental take" — called an *incidental take statement* (ITS) — that, among other things, sets out terms and conditions with which the federal agency (or applicant) must comply[27] and specifies "the procedures to be used to handle or dispose of any individuals of a species actually taken."[28]

Irrelevance of Cost and the Availability of Injunctive Relief

In *TVA v. Hill*,[29] the Supreme Court held that the statutory language does not allow a district court to consider cost in deciding whether to grant injunctive relief in the face of an ESA violation. There, environmental groups challenged the completion of a dam on the ground that the use of the dam would affect the habitat of an endangered snail darter. Rejecting the argument that the $80 million already spent on the dam justified completing the project, the Court ruled that considerations of cost lay beyond the scope of analysis called for by the act. Importantly, the Court also held that injunctive relief was available to remedy violations of section 7 and that it was mandated where violation of the act was shown.

Exemptions from ESA Coverage

Congress responded to the Court's *TVA v. Hill* decision by amending the ESA to create a committee empowered to exempt particular projects from ESA coverage. This committee, commonly referred to as the *God Squad* (because of its power to determine the fate of endangered and threatened species), consists of seven members: the secretaries of agriculture, of the interior, and of the army; the chair of the President's Council of Economic Advisers; the EPA Administrator; the administrator of the National Oceanic and Atmospheric Administration; and a representative from the affected state appointed by the President.[30] Federal agencies have only rarely turned to the God Squad for relief. And the God Squad has never permitted a federal agency to wipe out an entire species.

National security concerns can trump the ESA. First, the God Squad committee must grant an exemption from ESA coverage "if the Secretary of Defense finds that such exemption is necessary for reasons of national security."[31] A statute Congress enacted in 2005 vests exempting authority in the secretary of homeland security. The Real ID Act of 2005 — so named because of restrictions that other provisions of that act impose on states in issuing drivers' licenses — empowers the secretary of homeland security to waive any law (including the ESA) that the secretary "determines necessary to ensure expeditious construction of the barriers and roads" necessary for national security purposes.[32] As you may have read, the secretary recently used this authority to facilitate construction of the national border fence along the U.S.–Mexican border in the southwestern United States.

Restrictions on Public and Private Actions

Section 9 of the act provides numerous restrictions, which apply to both private and public actors. The most important of these is the provision making it unlawful to "take" any endangered species of fish or wildlife.[33] (Note that this restriction on its face does not apply to threatened animal species at all or to either endangered or threatened species of plants. However, as discussed shortly, agency regulations generally extend the section 9 restrictions to threatened animal species.) The use of the word *take* may strike readers as mysterious and leave them wondering exactly what the statute is aiming to prohibit. The act broadly defines *take* to mean "to harass, harm, pursue, hunt, shoot, wound, kill, trap, capture, or collect, or to attempt to engage in any such conduct."[34] One can readily see a common string running through all these words — the regulation clearly seeks to prohibit actual harm coming to a member of an endangered species. Other actions may indirectly harm the viability of an endangered species. Consider development of property that removes critical habitat and affects the ability of the species to procreate. Does such an action fall within the prohibition?

An ESA regulation answers this question in the affirmative. It defines *harm* as used in the elucidation of *take* in the preceding regulation to include any "significant habitat modification or degradation [that] actually kills or injures wildlife by significantly impairing essential behavioral patterns, including breeding, feeding, or sheltering."[35] In *Babbitt v. Sweet Home Chapter of Communities for a Greater Oregon*,[36] the Supreme Court upheld the validity of this regulation.

Protection of Endangered Plants

We observed earlier that the prohibition against taking endangered species does not apply to endangered species of plants. The only broadly applicable limitation found in section 9 applicable to endangered plant species is the restriction against removing, digging, cutting up, or damaging or destroying such species.[37]

Protection of Threatened Species

The section 9 statutory prohibitions do not apply to species listed as only threatened. Another provision of the act allows agencies by regulation to protect threatened species.[38] Both the FWS and NMFS have issued generic regulations that afford all the protections that section 9 provides to endangered species in turn to threatened species, except to the extent that the relevant agency promulgates a rule applicable to a particular threatened species. The default rule, then, is that threatened species receive the same protections as endangered species.

Incidental Take Permits

In 1982, Congress sought to mitigate the harsh results of application of section 9 by authorizing the promulgation of incidental take permits (ITPs). Section 10 of the act authorizes agencies to issue such permits, and thus to authorize an action that section 9 would otherwise prohibit as a take, only if the authorized take is "incidental to, and not the purpose of, the carrying out of an otherwise lawful activity."[39] A second prerequisite is that the applicant submit a so-called *habitat conservation plan* for the relevant species that specifies (1) the likely impact of the taking that would be authorized, (2) steps the applicant will undertake to minimize and mitigate that impact, and (3) possible alternatives that the applicant considered and the reasons why those alternatives were not chosen.[40] Before issuing an incidental take permit, the agency must be able to conclude that the take to be authorized "will not appreciably reduce the likelihood of survival and recovery of the species in the wild."[41]

CHAPTER RECAP

What have we learned in this chapter? The ESA protects endangered and protected species of flora and fauna.

Decisions to list species as either endangered or threatened (or to delist or downlist species) are undertaken by the FWS or NMFS, as appropriate. The statute directs the government to rely on the best available science in making listing decisions and designating critical habitats.

Once a species is listed as endangered or threatened, the federal government must ensure that its actions do not jeopardize the existence of that species. The Supreme Court has held that costs of compliance are not a relevant consideration in undertaking this obligation.

The ESA also limits private parties' freedom to take actions that take endangered animal species. The Supreme Court has upheld regulations that extend the scope of the limitations to actions that may interfere with a species' ability to reproduce. Private parties may seek an incidental take permit in order to engage in activities that may incidentally result in the take of some members of an endangered species.

ENDNOTES

1. 16 U.S.C. §§1531–1599.
2. ESA §3(6), 16 U.S.C. §1532(6).
3. *Id.* §4, 16 U.S.C. §1533.
4. *Id.* §3(6), 16 U.S.C. §1532(6).
5. *Id.* §3(20), 16 U.S.C. §1532(20).
6. *Id.* §4(a)(1), 16 U.S.C. §1533(a)(1).
7. *Id.* §4(b), 16 U.S.C. §1533(b)
8. *Id.* §3(16), 16 U.S.C. §1532(16).
9. *Id.* §4(a)(3), 16 U.S.C. §1533(a)(3).
10. *Id.*
11. *Id.* §4(b)(2), 16 U.S.C. §1533(b)(2).
12. *Id.* §4(b)(3), 16 U.S.C. §1533(b)(3).
13. *Id.* §7(a)(1), 16 U.S.C. §1536(a)(1).
14. *Id.* §7(a)(4), 16 U.S.C. §1536(a)(4).
15. *Id.* §7(a)(2), 16 U.S.C. §1536(a)(2).
16. *See* 50 C.F.R. §402.14(a).
17. *See* ESA §7(c), 15 U.S.C. §1536(c).
18. 50 C.F.R. §402.14(b)(1).
19. *Id.* §402.14(b)(2).
20. *Id.* §402.14(g)(1).
21. *Id.* §402.14(g)(2).

22. *Id.* §402.14(g)(3).

23. *Id.* §402.14(g)(4).

24. *Id.* §402.14(g)(5).

25. *Id.*

26. ESA §7(b)(4), 15 U.S.C. §1536(b)(4); 50 C.F.R. §402.14(i)(1).

27. 50 C.F.R. §402.14(i)(1)(4).

28. *Id.* §402.14(i)(1)(5).

29. 437 U.S. 153 (1978).

30. ESA §7(e), 16 U.S.C. §1536(e). An exemption requires the superma-jority vote of at least five members of the committee. Interestingly, although it was created by Congress in response to the Court's decision in *Hill*, the God Squad voted to deny an exemption to the dam that was at issue in *Hill*. Congress provided a specific statutory exception thereafter.

31. *Id.* §7(j), 16 U.S.C. §1536(j).

32. Pub. L. No. 104-208, 104th Cong., §102 (2005) (codified as a Note following 8 U.S.C. §1103). An earlier statute already conveyed similar authority on the attorney general to waive application of the ESA and NEPA.

33. ESA §9(a)(1)(B), 16 U.S.C. §1538(a)(1)(B).

34. *Id.* §3(19), 16 U.S.C. §1532(19).

35. 50 C.F.R. 17.3.

36. 515 U.S. 687 (1995).

37. ESA §9(a)(2)(B), 16 U.S.C. §1538(a)(2)(B).

38. *Id.* §4(b), 16 U.S.C. §1533(b).

39. *Id.* §10(a)(1)(B), 16 U.S.C. §1539(a)(1)(B).

40. *Id.* §10(a)(2)(A), 16 U.S.C. §1539(a)(2)(A).

41. *Id.* §10(a)(2)(B)(iv), 16 U.S.C. §1539(a)(2)(B)(iv).

~ 7 ~

Introducing Environmental Concerns to Government Decision Making: NEPA

I n this chapter, we shall consider information-forcing statutes — that is, environmental regulations that do not directly produce a particular environmentally friendly outcome but simply mandate that information be generated. Our focus will be on the National Environmental Policy Act of 1970 (NEPA),[1] although we will also briefly consider a couple of other provisions that rely on information-based regulation.

NEPA — INTRODUCTION

NEPA directs that when a major federal action may significantly affect the quality of the human environment, the relevant agency must prepare an *environmental impact statement* (EIS). As we shall see, the EIS should discuss how the proposed

action will affect the environment, consider possible alternatives to the proposed action that may be less environmentally
damaging, and set out mitigating steps that will be undertaken.
However, the statute does not direct that the agency that
prepares the EIS thereafter must reach an outcome that is
more favorable to the environment. Indeed, though the statute
requires the agency to prepare an EIS, and, technically, the
agency may have to read the EIS and state that it was considered,[2] there is no requirement that the EIS in the end have any
effect on agency decision making. As the Supreme Court
clearly held in *Strycker's Bay Neighborhood Council v. Karlen*,[3]
NEPA does not require that the agency actually consider the
contents of the EIS in reaching its final determination.

You may recall from our discussion in Chapter 1 that the
effectiveness of information-forcing statutes is controversial.
After all, such statutes do not mandate environmentally friendly
outcomes. How, then, can they be considered to be effective?

Many commentators believe that the statute needs stronger
teeth. That said, NEPA does have some teeth, and it is important to understand those teeth.

First, the mere effort of gathering and organizing information may have an effect on the decision maker. Even decision
makers who are not inherently favorably disposed to environmental concerns may have a change of heart when specific
information about harm to the environment is directly under
their noses.

A different take focuses on the interplay among information
dissemination, the public, and government decision makers.
Even if decision makers are not swayed by information about a
project's deleterious environmental effects, the public at large
may be. And decision makers may face pressure from the
public to factor environmental concerns into their decision
making. As we shall discuss shortly, compliance with NEPA
and issuance of an EIS contemplates considerable public
involvement. Even officials who are not directly elected may

feel pressure from elected officials to moderate their decision making.

Third, even if one does not believe that an EIS would actually change a decision maker's mind, NEPA may still have a substantive effect. Consider that preparing an EIS entails substantial money and time. Moreover, agency compliance with NEPA is subject to judicial review. Policymakers may choose to scale back projects, and thus also to reduce environmental impacts, so as to avoid the strictures of the EIS in the first place. On the other hand, if the agency does go forward with an EIS, the time that NEPA and judicial review buys may be enough for additional information to come to light, or for a change in administration — and decision maker.[4]

OVERVIEW OF NEPA PROCEDURE

NEPA is often described as a procedural statute. How does NEPA procedure work? Although we will discuss that procedure in detail shortly, an introductory overview is appropriate. First, the NEPA regulatory scheme is promulgated not by the Environmental Protection Agency (EPA), but by the White House Council on Environmental Quality (CEQ). These regulations effectively mediate between EPA and other federal agencies that are undertaking actions — sometimes called *action agencies* — that may trigger NEPA.

Before a government agency undertakes a major federal action, it must determine whether the action will significantly affect the human environment. If so, then the agency must prepare an EIS. How, then, does the agency decide whether there is a significant effect? The possible situations fall into three categories.[5]

First, an agency may be confident that both of these requirements are met. In such instances, the agency will simply prepare an EIS.

Second, an agency that is unsure whether an EIS will be necessary will undertake a preliminary environmental study. This is called an *environmental assessment* (EA). The EA is a shorter, more cursory EIS. If the EA reveals that a significant effect is likely, then the agency must prepare an EIS. If not, then the agency issues a *finding of no significant impact* (FONSI). The FONSI reflects the agency's conclusion that preparation of an EIS is unnecessary.

Third, some actions are exempt from the requirement of preparing an EA or an EIS. CEQ regulations provide for *categorical exclusions*. These are "actions which do not individually or cumulatively have a significant effect on the human environment and which have been found to have no such effect in procedures adopted by a Federal agency in implementation of these regulations . . . and for which, therefore, neither an environmental assessment nor an environmental impact statement is required."[6]

In addition, there are statutory exceptions to NEPA. Decisions under the Clean Air Act are specifically exempted from the purview of NEPA,[7] and many Clean Water Act decisions are also exempted.[8] Further, the secretary of homeland security is granted the unilateral power to exempt decisions from NEPA's scope as he or she "determines necessary to ensure expeditious construction of the barriers and roads" necessary to attain border security.[9] The secretary recently invoked this power in connection with the construction of a border fence along the U.S.–Mexico border.

Public involvement is an integral part of the NEPA process. And judicial review of an agency's FONSI decision is available, as is review of agency EAs and EISs.

WHEN MUST AN EIS BE PREPARED?

NEPA directs that an EIS must be prepared whenever two conditions are present. First, there must be a "major federal action." Second, that major federal action must "significantly affect the human environment." We shall consider each condition in turn. As we shall see, the first condition is more straightforward than the second.

What Is a Major Federal Action?

How can we decide whether a government action constitutes a major federal action? A CEQ regulation explains that the term "includes actions with effects that may be major and which are potentially subject to Federal control and responsibility."[10] Actions are defined to "include new and continuing activities, including projects and programs entirely or partly financed, assisted, conducted, regulated, or approved by federal agencies; new or revised agency rules, regulations, plans, policies, or procedures; and legislative proposals."[11] The regulation also explains that federal actions will "tend" to be one of the following: adoption of official policy, adoption of formal plans, adoption of programs ("such as a group of concerted actions to implement a specific policy or plan"), and approval of specific projects.[12] Note that the last category, approval of projects, includes "actions approved by permit or other regulatory decision as well as federal and federally assisted activities."[13]

The remaining issue here is the definition of *major*. The CEQ regulation instructs that that term "reinforces but does not have a meaning independent" of the term *significantly*[14] — which regulations in turn define in terms of the "context" and "intensity" of the proposed action.[15] It seems clear that the larger the project is, in terms of resources involved and scope of impact, the more likely that the project will be considered major. It is important not to focus too heavily on the scope of the finished project, lest one lose sight of the scope of the effort and resources (and impact) needed to effectuate the project.

The importance of classifying a project as major invites those who want to undertake a project with the costs and potential difficulties associated with preparing an EIS to "frame" the project so as to make it seem less major. Consider that a single project is likely to sound far more major than is a description of four smaller projects that, taken together, are equivalent to the single large project.

As an example, let us say that an agency is contemplating opening a portion of a national forest to the timber industry. To do so, it plans to construct a road into the forest. Construction of the road itself may not be a major action, but completion of the road will facilitate timber industry access to the forest; indeed, there is no other reason to build the road. May the agency frame the project simply as one to construct the road, and leave until later (including preparation of an EIS) the rest of the plan? Courts have held that the agency must treat the entire project as a whole; segmentation is not allowed. NEPA regulations, issued by the President's Council on Environmental Quality, today confirm this interpretation.

When Does a Major Federal Action Significantly Affect the Human Environment? — Substance

Let us consider the substantive question of how to decide whether a major federal action "significantly affects the human environment." This entails understanding what an effect is, when an effect is significant, and also what constitutes the human environment.

We begin with the interpretation of *human environment.* The term has been interpreted more broadly than one perhaps ordinarily understands it. A CEQ regulation instructs that *human environment* be "interpreted comprehensively to include the natural and physical environment and the relationship of people with that environment."[16] Thus, although "economic or social effects are not intended by themselves to require preparation of an environmental impact statement," still "[w]hen an environmental impact statement is prepared and economic or social and natural or physical environmental effects are interrelated, then the environmental impact statement will discuss all of these effects on the human environment."[17] For example, if the federal action is construction of a building that will house a detention center in a major urban area, then it may be important to consider the effects of the project on traffic and crime. The question of what exactly will be considered components of the human environment will vary with the particular context.

A CEQ regulation explains that (consistent with the broad understanding of *human environment*) *effects* — which is coextensive with *impacts* — include "ecological (such as the effects on natural resources and on the components, structures, and functioning of affected ecosystems), aesthetic, historic, cultural, economic, social, or health, whether direct, indirect, or cumulative."[18]

Effect is intended to encompass both direct and indirect effects.[19] Direct effects "are caused by the action and occur at the same time and place,"[20] whereas indirect effects "are caused by the action and are later in time or farther removed in distance, but are still reasonably foreseeable."[21] Again, consistent with the broad understanding of *human environment*, the regulation explains that "[i]ndirect effects may include growth inducing effects and other effects related to induced changes in the pattern of land use, population density or growth rate, and related effects on air and water and other natural systems, including ecosystems."[22]

In deciding whether an impact is significant, courts have pointed to two factors to consider: the cumulative impact and the marginal impact. A project could have a significant overall impact — that is, that the project itself could be large. And even if the effect of the project itself is not very large, it may, when combined with preexisting conditions, "tip the scales" such that the environmental impact will exceed the project's marginal contribution.

The CEQ regulations confirm this approach. They direct that agencies consider the "context" and "intensity" of the proposed action.[23] The inclusion of *context* as a factor confirms that although the impact of a project in one area may not be significant, the impact of a similar project in another, more environmentally sensitive area may be.

The framing question that we discussed earlier in the context of whether there is a major federal action looms large as well in the context of whether there is a *significant impact*. Recall the earlier example in which the environmental impact of the construction of a single road is dwarfed by the environmental impact of opening up a national forest to the timber industry. Accordingly, courts and CEQ regulations generally require agencies to treat projects that are interrelated as one. They also resist allowing agencies to treat projects that would not be undertaken without other steps to be treated independently of those other steps. Thus, for example, the construction of a causeway to an island should be considered part and parcel with plans to develop the island if the causeway would not be constructed were it not for a desire to develop the island. At the same time, courts give agencies flexibility in deciding how to structure regulatory steps and will not second-guess an agency's decision to take steps that are not inherently interdependent separately.[24]

When Does a Major Federal Action Significantly Affect the Human Environment? — Procedure

As noted earlier in the NEPA overview, the procedural device by which the agency examines whether a project will result in a significant impact on the environment is an environmental assessment (EA). The conclusion that the impact will not be significant is called a finding of no significant impact (FONSI).

If an agency cannot reach a FONSI based on the EA, it then prepares an EIS. Public involvement can be expected along the way, especially if the project is controversial. The agency often issues a draft EIS, on which public comments are solicited. Based on those comments, the agency may amend the draft EIS. Ultimately, the agency issues a final EIS. At this point, the agency's actions are subject to judicial review. (If the agency issued a FONSI, then that conclusion, and the adequacy of the EA, is subject to judicial review at that point.)

The EA is essentially a streamlined EIS. Although we have yet to discuss exactly what a satisfactory EIS should contain, the EA requires similar content, only less detailed discussion. Some public attention and involvement is also likely. If the agency must prepare an EA anyway and the EA has the same content as an EIS, why not just prepare an EIS in the first place? The answer is that the full requirements of an EIS are *much* more demanding than those of an EA, in terms again of both cost and time. Thus, in general, an agency skips the EA stage only when it is already certain that it must prepare a full-fledged EIS.

TIMING OF THE EIS

If the EIS is to have any substantive effect at all, then it must be completed before the agency decides to proceed with the project. Put another way, the chance that consideration of an EIS may affect a decision is surely much larger before lots of money and time have been invested in a project. Thus, it is important that an EIS be completed before the initial decision-making process.

This goal again highlights the importance of segmenting projects for NEPA purposes. (Recall the earlier discussion of agency freedom to treat different regulatory steps separately.) If a project can be broken into pieces, each of which gets separate NEPA consideration over a period of time, then it is far more likely that each individual segment will not warrant an EIS. It may also be more likely that, once earlier segments have been studied and approved, it will be practically more difficult to reject a later segment, even if the EIS accompanying that segment raises serious environmental concerns.

EIS ADEQUACY

What should a properly prepared EIS contain? How can we judge its adequacy? In general, courts understand NEPA and the regulations thereunder to be governed by a *rule of reason*[25] — that is, the EIS must be reasonable in light of the circumstances. Beyond this, we may think of four possible considerations: contents, context, time and effort, and bad faith.

Consider contents first. The statute and CEQ regulations identify certain items that an EIS should contain. These include a statement of the purpose of and need for the action; a description of possible alternatives, including a discussion of why those alternatives are not preferable; a statement of the environmental impact of the action; and a recitation of measures that may be taken to mitigate that impact.

If an EIS is missing any of these items, it will be deemed inadequate. In how much depth, however, must the EIS discuss any of these points? This is where the second consideration, context, comes into play. What may be relevant for discussion in the context of one project may not be so relevant for discussion in the context of another.

Let us consider the EIS section devoted to a discussion of the possible alternatives. CEQ regulations and, often, court decisions focus on this as an especially important EIS section.

An agency is expected to identify other ways to achieve the same goal with less of an environmental impact. Needless to say, theoretically one may think to discuss many different alternatives. Courts apply the rule of reason to the discussion of alternatives: Agencies need not discuss every possible alternative, but rather only those that are realistically possible. Courts generally require the federal agency to identify and discuss a range of possible alternatives that are reasonable in the particular context. For example, an alternative to constructing a new power plant pertaining to energy conservation may be more relevant in a time when energy costs are high than when they are not. Finally, the agency must discuss the *no-action alternative* — that is, the possibility of taking no action.

What if a third party believes that there is an alternative that the agency has not considered but should? Recall that the NEPA procedure contemplates public involvement. The third party should raise that alternative as part of that process. Then, if the agency does not respond to the point, the agency's action may be subject to judicial challenge. Put another way, points raised by the public may require agency attention even if the point otherwise would not have had to be covered by the agency in the final EIS.

What if the point is never raised by the third party during public proceedings but is then raised by the third party as part of a judicial challenge to the agency's final EIS? Here, courts may rule that the argument is procedurally improper; the third party may have waived the argument by failing to raise it in a timely manner during public proceedings before issuance of the final EIS. Put another way, unless there is some reason explaining the failure to raise the point earlier (perhaps new circumstances have made it relevant), the agency's EIS will be considered adequately prepared in light of the circumstances at the time. An agency deserves notice of the grounds on which an EIS will be challenged.

An EIS is often a lengthy document that has taken a long time to prepare. Even a well-prepared document may not be perfect, however. Some courts have exhibited a willingness nonetheless to accept such EISs as adequate, in light of the substantial good-faith effort put forth by the agency. A few errors or omissions among thousands of pages will not doom an EIS to a finding of inadequacy.

At the same time, nothing may be more likely to make a court conclude that an EIS is inadequate than a finding by the court that the agency acted in bad faith. For example, one court invalidated an EIS on the ground that the relevant agency deliberately overlooked pertinent scientific studies and the input of a sibling federal agency.[26]

OTHER FEDERAL INFORMATION-BASED REGULATORY PROVISIONS

A few other federal statutes include provisions that rely on information to achieve regulatory goals. Note that, unlike NEPA, these statutes involve disclosure of information with respect to either private actors or states.

The Emergency Planning and Community Right-to-Know Act of 1986 (EPCRA)[27] requires companies to disclose to EPA when they have released toxic chemicals. From these reports, EPA assembles the *toxic release inventory* (TRI). The TRI has been successful; no company wants to find itself near the top of the TRI. The statute provides a good example of how information can combine with public pressure to effect environmental change in the absence of substantive regulation.

In addition, the Clean Water Act calls for states to report to EPA the water quality of all water bodies within their borders, including identification of all water bodies not in compliance with existing water quality standards.[28]

CHAPTER RECAP

What have we learned in this chapter? NEPA requires the government to consider explicitly environmental concerns and ramifications of certain decisions. NEPA's requirements are purely procedural, not substantive — that is, they require the government only to make itself aware of environmental concerns, not to reach any particular outcome with respect to, or based on, them. That said, it is often argued that awareness of issues sometimes has an impact on final government decisions. NEPA may also affect government decision making a little more indirectly insofar as NEPA calls for public involvement in the preparation and release of the government's findings.

NEPA applies to major federal actions that may have a significant effect on the environment. The government decides whether an action will have a significant effect by preparing an environmental assessment (EA). If the government concludes that the action will not have a significant impact, then it issues a finding of no significant impact (FONSI). If it concludes otherwise, then it must issue an environmental impact statement (EIS). Issuances of FONSIs and the adequacy of EAs and EISs are subject to judicial review.

The government may be able to manipulate whether a project is major and whether a project's impact will be significant by framing the project broadly or narrowly. Regulations and court decisions endeavor to limit the government's discretion in this regard.

ENDNOTES

1. 42 U.S.C. §§4321–4370f.
2. *See Calvert Cliffs' Coordinating Committee v. U.S. Atomic Energy Commn.*, 449 F.2d 1109 (D.C. Cir. 1971).
3. 444 U.S. 223 (1980) (per curiam).
4. You might consider the magnitude of the possible effects discussed in the text in the context of a 2008 decision by the Ninth Circuit, which required the

National Highway Traffic Safety Administration to consider the effects of global warming under NEPA in setting fuel economy standards for motor vehicles. *See Center for Biological Diversity v. National Highway Traffic Safety Admin.*, 538 F.3d 1172 (9th Cir. 2008).

5. *See* 40 C.F.R. §1501.4.

6. *Id.* §1508.4.

7. *See* 15 U.S.C. §793(c)(1).

8. *See* Clean Water Act §511(c), 33 U.S.C. §1369(c).

9. *See supra* note 16 in Chapter 6. As mentioned there, an earlier statute already gave the attorney general similar authority to waive application of the ESA and NEPA.

10. 40 C.F.R. §1508.18.

11. *Id.*

12. *Id.*

13. *Id.*

14. *Id.*

15. *Id.* §1508.27.

16. *Id.* §1508.14.

17. *Id.*

18. *Id.* §1508.8.

19. *Id.*

20. *Id.* §1508.8(a).

21. *Id.* §1508.8(b).

22. *Id.*

23. *Id.* §1508.27.

24. *See Kleppe v. Sierra Club*, 427 U.S. 390 (1976).

25. *See, e.g., Dep't of Transp. v. Public Citizen*, 541 U.S. 752, 767 (2004).

26. *See Sierra Club v. U.S. Army Corps of Engineers*, 701 F.2d 1011 (2d Cir. 1983).

27. 42 U.S.C. §§11001–11050.

28. *See* Clean Water Act §305, 33 U.S.C. §1315.

⁓ 8 ⁓

Methods of Enforcement

In this chapter, we will survey various ways that the Environmental Protection Agency (EPA; or some other relevant agency) can be compelled to administer the environmental laws. We will begin with an examination of the tools available to the government to pursue those who allegedly violate the environmental laws.

After that, we will explore private rights of action — generally called *citizen suits* — both against EPA and against those alleged to have violated an environmental law. We will consider provisions in the environmental laws that give rise to private rights of action. We will also consider the notion of *standing* as an extrastatutory limit on private parties' ability to bring citizen suits, as well as a limit on congressional power to confer statutory standing.

Finally, we will conclude with consideration of executive and legislative abilities to control the actions of EPA.

GOVERNMENT ENFORCEMENT OF THE ENVIRONMENTAL LAWS AGAINST ALLEGED VIOLATORS

The government has several tools at its disposal to enforce the federal environmental laws against alleged violators: administrative enforcement, civil enforcement, and criminal enforcement. Each of these tools has its own procedures and provides different remedies against violators. We discuss each in turn.

Before proceeding, however, it is important to note that each environmental statute has its own enforcement provisions. These provisions are not uniform. In the discussion that follows, we survey the statutory regimes in general and point out a few specific examples. It is imperative that you acquaint yourself with the particular statute at issue in a given situation in order to understand what specific rules apply.

Administrative Enforcement

Administrative enforcement is the most common method by which the government enforces environmental laws against alleged violators. Some statutes allow EPA to seek modest monetary penalties through administrative enforcement. For example, Clean Air Act and Clean Water Act enforcement penalties are subject to a cap.[1] EPA also may seek to terminate, suspend, or revoke a relevant permit. Administrative enforcement actions proceed initially before EPA (or another government department, as in the case of the Endangered Species Act — ESA),[2] with appeals generally occurring in federal court.[3] When a state is deputized to administer part of a federal statutory program — as under the Clean Water Act — then the state may bring its own enforcement proceedings, with the federal government stepping in to the extent that the state fails to enforce on its own.[4]

Civil Enforcement

EPA may seek monetary penalties, and also temporary and permanent injunctive relief, in a civil enforcement proceeding. These proceedings are brought in federal district court.

Calculating Penalties

Monetary penalties for violation of the environmental laws generally may be obtained by EPA in either administrative or civil proceedings.[5] These penalties are calculated by reference to the governing statute and may accrue on a daily basis.[6] Among the factors that are typically considered in setting penalties are considerations of justice, the size of the business in question and the economic impact of the penalty on the business, the violator's compliance history and prior good-faith efforts to comply, the duration of the violation, and the seriousness of the violation.[7]

EPA has promulgated policies governing the calculation of civil penalties under the Clean Water Act and Clean Air Act. In assessing penalties, courts usually take either a *top-down* or *bottom-up* approach. Under a top-down approach, the court begins with the maximum allowable statutory penalty and then uses relevant factors to adjust the penalty down as appropriate. Under a "bottom-up" approach, the court instead begins with the economic benefit the defendant derived from the violation in question — which is generally one of the factors to be used in determining the proper sanction — and then looks to the remaining factors to determine whether adjustments up or down are appropriate.

Criminal Enforcement

The federal environmental laws and criminal code empower the government to pursue criminal cases against those who knowingly, recklessly, or negligently violate certain provisions of the federal environmental laws.[8] The most serious crimes, and the ones that subject those convicted to the most severe punishments, are *knowing endangerment* crimes — that is, crimes in which the defendant knowingly put others in danger by virtue of his or her behavior.[9]

Those convicted of environmental crimes may have to pay criminal fines and could face imprisonment. Criminal prosecutions are brought in federal district court and are usually prosecuted by the local U.S. attorney's office. Defendants in criminal prosecutions for violations of the environmental laws are entitled to all the protections enjoyed by all criminal defendants. In particular, violations must be proven beyond a reasonable doubt. Criminal prosecutions for environmental law violations have been to date uncommon.

CITIZEN SUITS — INTRODUCTION

In addition to introducing much in the way of substantive laws to protect the environment, the environmental laws of the 1970s included another important innovation: the private right of action or, more commonly, the *citizen suit*. The U.S. Congress chose to empower private citizens to bring suit and enforce the environmental laws for two reasons. First, Congress was concerned that special interests might successfully co-opt EPA and prevent it from fulfilling its obligations and enforcing the laws. Second, Congress sought to democratize the environmental laws by involving the citizenry in their enforcement. Today, the citizen suit is emulated in other statutes, both domestically and in environmental statutes abroad.

As alluded to in Chapter 2, the Administrative Procedure Act (APA) authorizes certain private challenges to governmental administrative actions. Beyond this, every major environmental statute with the exception of FIFRA features a citizen suit provision. These provisions go beyond the APA and authorize private societal actors to bring two kinds of suits. First, they may sue EPA (or other relevant federal agency) for failing to fulfill a nondiscretionary duty under the environmental statute in question. Second, acting as so-called *private attorneys general*, they may sue any public or private actor alleged to be in violation of the environmental statute. We consider each of these types of private rights of action in turn. After that, we will address the question of *standing*, which plaintiffs must meet even if they meet the requirements of the statute authorizing private rights of action.

Citizen Suits Against EPA

The authority to bring private actions is not restricted to individuals. Public interest organizations, corporations, and even states and municipalities may all do so.

Challenges by private actors against EPA fall into two categories. First, private actors may bring suit in federal court against EPA to compel it to live up to its obligations under an environmental statute. Actionable obligations are those that create a *nondiscretionary duty* in EPA. A nondiscretionary duty is one over which EPA does not have discretion — that is, any freedom to exercise its own judgment — over whether to take action. Under the relevant statute, EPA is obligated either to act or not to act, and the challenger asserts that EPA has not lived up to its duty. The paradigmatic of such a duty is an obligation on which Congress has imposed on EPA a statutory deadline by which it must comply. Thus, for example, environmental organizations have sued EPA numerous times — often successfully — to compel the agency to issue effluent limitations under the Clean Water Act when EPA had missed statutory deadlines by which it was supposed to have acted. Note that the private actor may have to give EPA notice of the violation and wait some period of time to see whether the violation is remedied before filing suit.

Environmental statutes generally also authorize private actors to sue EPA to challenge certain regulations promulgated under each statute. Here, the actors may argue, for example, that a regulation promulgated by EPA does not conform to the terms of the governing statutory provision (as discussed in Chapter 2).

Recall that EPA may also issue a regulation in an adjudicative capacity, for example, to resolve a petition; here, as well, private actors may challenge the resulting order. A recent and much heralded example of such a suit is the Supreme Court case of *Massachusetts v. EPA*.[10] There, several states and municipalities joined environmental organizations in challenging EPA's order, which rejected their petition to have it regulate greenhouse gas emissions from motor vehicles.

Citizen Suits Against Violators

As is the case for private actions against EPA, the authority to bring private actions against violators of environmental laws is not restricted to individuals. Public interest organizations, corporations, and even states and municipalities may all do so.

Under the Clean Air Act, no private action against a violator may be maintained if either EPA or the state in whose jurisdiction the violator lies "has commenced and is diligently prosecuting a civil action in a court of the United States or a State to require compliance."[11] If there is no such action, then the private actor must first provide "notice of the violation" to EPA, to the state in whose jurisdiction the violator lies, and to the violator.[12] Then, after a period of time to allow for remedy of the violation and/or prosecution by EPA or the state, the private actor may file its lawsuit in federal district court.[13]

Prior to 1990, the citizen suit provisions of the various environmental statutes contained language typified by this provision still applicable under the Clean Water Act: Suit is permitted "against any person . . . alleged to be in violation" of a Clean Water Act effluent standard or EPA or state order with respect to such a standard.[14] In its 1987 decision in *Gwaltney of Smithfield, Ltd. v. Chesapeake Bay Foundation*, the Supreme Court ruled that the language "alleged to be in violation" in the Clean Air Act should be interpreted to require a "state of either continuous or intermittent violation." At the least, then, a plaintiff had to establish "a reasonable likelihood that a past polluter will continue to pollute in the future."[15] This interpretation forecloses suits alleging only past violations.[16]

In response to this decision, Congress amended the relevant Clean Air Act provision specifically to authorize citizen suits against defendants "alleged to have violated (if there is evidence that the alleged violation has been repeated) or to be in violation" of the act.[17] Congress did not amend the citizen suit provisions in other environmental statutes, however, and the Court's decision in *Gwaltney* presumably applies to those that still employ the present tense — such as the Clean Water Act — as the Clean Air Act used to.

Civil penalties imposed upon a finding of violation in a private action are paid by the violator to the U.S. Treasury. To enhance the incentives for private actors to bring suit against violators, Congress has empowered courts to order defendants who lose to reimburse plaintiffs for their litigation costs, including their "reasonable" attorneys' fees.

There are exceptions to private parties' ability to bring lawsuits as private attorneys general. First, the Eleventh Amendment of the U.S. Constitution affirms states' sovereign immunity to lawsuits. It precludes private lawsuits against state and subdivisions thereof for some environmental law violations. At the same time, the Court's holding in *Ex parte Young*[18] allows for actions against state actors in their official capacity to enjoin prospectively continuing violations of federal law. This doctrine thus enables effective enforcement of the laws against the states.

Second, Congress has exempted some obligations from the proper scope of such actions. As an example, Congress has waived sovereign immunity for suits brought against EPA, but not the U.S. Army Corps of Engineers, for failure to comply with the strictures of the Clean Water Act.[19]

Third, Congress has seen fit to avoid the inconsistencies that might result from having public and private enforcement actions proceed at the same time. It thus has precluded private plaintiffs from filing suit if the federal or state government has commenced, or is "diligently prosecuting," either a criminal or civil action. Under some federal environmental statutes, some administrative enforcement proceedings will also suffice to preclude a citizen's suit. Beyond this, Congress has seen fit to give the federal government a "right of first refusal" of sorts in pursuing environmental violations. It thus has required prospective plaintiffs to give the federal government, any relevant state authority, and the alleged private violator at least 60 days' notice before filing suit. If any government commences an action within that time, the suit is barred; the would-be plaintiffs generally can join the government's lawsuit, however, as interveners-as-of-right. Most courts also hold that the entry of a consent decree also bars a private suit, even if no formal litigation is commenced by the government.

Standing

Standing doctrine, as developed by the Supreme Court, provides limits on when societal actors may pursue cases in federal court. Standing draws from both constitutional mandates — including the Article III requirement that federal courts hear only "cases and controversies" and concerns over separation of powers among the branches — and prudential concerns. For a plaintiff to pursue a case in federal court, the requirements of standing must be met. If they are not, then the case will not be heard, even if there is a statutory provision that otherwise would authorize such a lawsuit.

At the doctrine's base, the Court has interpreted standing to consist of three elements: *injury in fact, causation,* and *redressability.* Injury in fact requires the plaintiff to show that he, she, or it has actually been injured; the relevant injury, it has been held, must be "actual" and "imminent." Causation requires that the plaintiff's injury be traceable to some action by the defendant. Redressability requires that some relief from the court will address remedy or ameliorate the plaintiff's injury.

The injury-in-fact requirement has been the source of the greatest controversy over the years. In *Sierra Club v. Morton,*[20] the Court held that the injury required need not be economic, but could involve aesthetic, conservational, and recreational values. The Court's ultimate holding in the case reflects standing doctrine's rigidity: The Court rejected an environmental organization's standing to challenge the Forest Service's decision to allow private development of a ski resort in a national forest on the ground that there was no specific allegation that any member of the organization had suffered aesthetic harm (a shortcoming that was remedied by the organization on refiling after dismissal). Similarly, in *Lujan v. Defenders of Wildlife,*[21] the Court found that an environmental organization lacked standing to challenge a governmental decision that the ESA does not apply to government actions that may affect endangered species overseas: Though two members of the group had previously traveled to the areas to be affected and expressed hope that they would return in the future, the Court found the absence of any definitive plan to return (including the purchase of air tickets) meant that the requirement that injury in fact be "actual and imminent" was not met.

The Court's decision in *Steel Co. v. Citizens for a Better Environment*[22] greatly restricts standing in federal court for cases alleging solely past violations of the environmental laws. The Court there ruled that a plaintiff environmental organization could not show the redressability necessary to support a challenge to an alleged past violation of the Emergency Planning and Community Right-to-Know Act of 1986. The Court rejected, among other things, the argument that penalties for past violations offered redress to the plaintiff, reasoning that because the penalties would be payable to the federal government and not to the plaintiff, the action for such penalties was better characterized as a general grievance.

In recent years, the Court has taken a more relaxed view of standing in environmental cases. In *Friends of the Earth, Inc. v. Laidlaw Environmental Services (TOC), Inc.*, the Court considered a private action by an environmental organization against a company for alleged Clean Water Act violations involving pollution discharges into a river. Emphasizing that "[t]he relevant showing for purposes of Article III standing, . . . is not injury to the environment but injury to the plaintiff," the Court upheld the organization's standing based on allegations that members of the organization had changed their behavior—for example, fished, hiked, and picnicked less—and had seen their properties decrease in value as a result of the alleged discharges.[23]

The Court's most recent statement on environmental standing comes from its decision in *Massachusetts v. EPA*. There, the Court found that Massachusetts had standing to challenge EPA's decision not to regulate motor vehicle tailpipe greenhouse gas emissions. The Court found sufficient evidence to support the plaintiffs' standing to bring suit the allegations—undisputed by EPA—that automobile emissions contributed to global warming and that global warming would cause Massachusetts to lose coastline. To the extent that the case came close to the line of proper standing, the Court noted that states seeking to protect their "quasi-sovereign interests" are "entitled to special solicitude in . . . standing analysis."[24]

EXECUTIVE AND LEGISLATIVE CONTROL OVER EPA

Our final topic is the question of how the executive and legislative branches exert control over — or, in effect, enforce their wishes against — EPA.

Executive Branch Control over EPA

The most apparent way that the executive branch can exert control over EPA is through the appointment process. The EPA Administrator and several other high-end positions at EPA are political appointments. Still, the vast bulk of work at EPA is conducted by career public servants who are not political appointees. Thus, the White House sometimes relies on other methods to rein in EPA discretion. One important tool is the use of executive orders. Among the subjects addressed by executive orders is a mandate that agencies rely on cost-benefit analysis. As discussed in Chapter 2, the White House Office of Management and Budget reviews regulations for compliance with cost-benefit analysis.

Legislative Branch Control over EPA

The legislature also has tools at its disposal to monitor EPA and hold it in check. The Senate's power to consent to presidential appointments is one such power. Second, both houses of the legislatures routinely hold oversight hearings at which EPA officials may testify. Third, Congress may specifically fund (or defund) particular EPA initiatives through its power over budget appropriations. Fourth, the legislature may include in statutes not just obligations on EPA, but timetables by which EPA is supposed to fulfill those obligations. The problem is that EPA sometimes fails to meet those obligations, and generally there is no mechanism (other than perhaps questions at an oversight hearing) to see that the obligations get done. One answer to this problem is the so-called *regulatory hammer* that Congress used in the context of the Solid Waste Disposal Act ban on landfills: As discussed in Chapter 5, Congress directed EPA to promulgate regulations detailing when wastes could be treated so as to "substantially diminish the toxicity of the waste" or the risk that hazardous constituents would migrate from a landfill in which they were disposed. Beyond this, moreover, Congress directed that, until EPA promulgated such regulations, there would be an absolute ban on land disposal. This had the effect of converting industrial actors that otherwise might have applauded delays on the part of EPA in promulgating such regulations into supporters of swift EPA action.

CHAPTER RECAP

What have we learned in this chapter? Congress has authorized private actors to sue to require EPA to meet its statutory obligations under many environmental statutes. It has also authorized private parties to sue for violations of many environmental statutes. Perhaps the largest barrier to private enforcement actions is the requirement that plaintiffs in such cases demonstrate standing to pursue them. The Court has interpreted the Constitution to require plaintiffs to show injury in fact; that the injury is caused by the defendant's action; and that a judicial remedy will redress the injury.

Both the legislature and the executive branch have ways to enforce their wills with respect to EPA. The legislature can limit agency discretion in its statutes. It can also exert its influence through the confirmation process for political appointees, through oversight hearings, and through appropriations. The executive controls agency discretion through political appointments.

ENDNOTES

1. *See, e.g.*, Clean Air Act §113(d)(1), 42 U.S.C. §7413(d)(1) (expressly providing that "[t]he Administrator's authority [to seek administrative penalties] shall be limited to matters where the total penalty sought does not exceed $200,000"); Clean Water Act §309(g)(2), 33 U.S.C. §1319(g)(2).

2. *See, e.g.*, Clean Water Act §309(a)(3), 33 U.S.C. §1319(a)(3); Clean Air Act §113(d), 42 U.S.C. §7413(d); ESA §11(a), 16 U.S.C. §1540(a).

3. *See, e.g., id.* §309(g)(8), 33 U.S.C. §1319(g)(8); Clean Air Act §113(d)(4), 42 U.S.C. §7413(d)(4). As a survey of these provisions reveals, the appropriate federal court (including whether the appeal should fall to a district court or a court of appeals) varies. The Endangered Species Act allows the appropriate government department to ask the attorney general to bring a civil suit in district court to the extent that an actor fails to pay an administrative penalty.

4. *See id.* §309(a)(1), (2), 33 U.S.C. §1319(a)(1), (2).

5. As we shall see shortly, private attorneys general may also secure monetary penalties against violators on behalf of the U.S. Treasury.

6. *See, e.g.*, Clean Air Act §113(c), (d); 42 U.S.C. §7413(c), (d) (establishing a daily monetary cap of $25,000 for violations).

7. *See, e.g., id.* §113(e)(1), 42 U.S.C. §7413(e)(1).

8. *See, e.g.*, Clean Water Act §309(c), 33 U.S.C. §1319(c); Clean Air Act §113(c), 42 U.S.C. §7413(c); ESA §11(b), 16 U.S.C. §1540(b).

9. *See* Clean Water Act §309(c)(3), 33 U.S.C. §1319(c)(3); Clean Air Act §113(c)(5), 42 U.S.C. §7413(c)(5).

10. 549 U.S. 497 (2007).

11. *See, e.g.*, Clean Air Act §304(b)(1)(B), 42 U.S.C. §7604(b)(1)(B). The provision goes on to provide that "in any such action in a [federal] court . . . any person may intervene as a matter of right." *Id.*

The Clean Water Act takes a similar approach, although it takes a more lenient approach with respect to certain violations, allowing citizen suits to be brought immediately with respect to such violations. *See* Clean Water Act §505(b), 33 U.S.C. §1365(b).

12. *See* Clean Air Act §304(b)(1)(A), 42 U.S.C. §7604(b)(1)(A).

13. *See id.*

14. Clean Water Act §505, 33 U.S.C. §1365.

15. 484 U.S. 49, 57 (1987).

16. Note also, as discussed shortly, that the Supreme Court's decision in *Steel Co. v. Citizens for a Better Environment*, 523 U.S. 83 (1998), greatly restricts standing in federal court for cases alleging solely past violations of the environmental laws.

17. Clean Air Act §304(a)(1), 42 U.S.C. §7604(a)(1).

18. 209 U.S. 123 (1908).

19. *See Alliance to Save the Mattaponi v. U.S. Army Corps of Engineers*, 515 F. Supp. 2d 1 (D.D.C. 2007).

20. 405 U.S. 727 (1972).

21. 504 U.S. 555 (1992).

22. 523 U.S. 83 (1998).

23. 528 U.S. 167, 181 (2000).

24. 549 U.S. at 520.

~ 9 ~

Regulation of the Environment at the International Level

International environmental law is a course, and whole area of study, unto itself. In this chapter, we will satisfy ourselves with a brief overview of the relevant issues, a summary discussion of a couple of treaty regimes, and an introduction to some elements of U.S. domestic law that implicate international issues.

THE GENESIS OF INTERNATIONAL ENVIRONMENTAL LAW

Let us begin by considering how international environmental law may differ from domestic environmental law. International environmental law is a subset of international law. Note that although we have a domestic government to generate domestic law, there is no analogous international government that generates international law. (The United Nations is as close as there is to an international government, and it does not generate binding international environmental law.)

In the absence of a government that can enact binding laws, when would you expect international environmental law to arise? The answer is that international environmental law arises by virtue of the agreement, or at least acquiescence, of the relevant parties.

There are two relevant sources of international environmental law: customary international law and treaty regimes.[1] Customary international law is perhaps most easily understood by focusing on the root word *custom*. It arises, in essence, when the nations of the world observe the legal principle at issue — in other words, when observing the principle becomes customary. Nations may expressly opt out of a particular customary international law; if they do not, however, then they are deemed to be bound.

Consider two problems with customary international law. First, it is amorphous. Insofar as it is not announced by treaty, one is left to find evidence of it by surveying state action or by referring to treatises by authors who purport to have surveyed state action. Second, consider the question of enforcement. Enforcement is always an issue in international law, but it is especially problematic with respect to customary law, in which the purportedly governing standard is often murky.

Is there any customary international environmental law? The two most prominent candidates are the precautionary principle and, less so, the "polluter pays" principle, both which were discussed in Chapter 1. The question of whether either of these principles constitutes customary international law remains subject to debate.

The other possible source of international environmental law is a treaty regime. A treaty regime will fall into one of three categories. A treaty between two nations is said to be *bilateral*. A treaty among some number of countries (usually in a region) is said to be *plurilateral*. Finally, a treaty that includes almost all of the world's nations is called *global regime*.

Needless to say, a treaty regime arises only by the agreement of the parties. Enforcement is an important issue for a treaty regime. The regime may provide for strong or weak methods of enforcement. Note that, irrespective of the enforcement mechanisms in the treaty, a party is always free simply to leave the treaty regime; this power influences the extent to which other parties may seek to have treaty obligations enforced.

INTERNATIONAL ENVIRONMENTAL TREATY REGIMES

There are international treaty regimes that address water pollution, biodiversity, trade in endangered species, and interstate transport of hazardous wastes, just to name a few. We will quickly look at two important international treaty regimes that address problems of air pollution: ozone depletion and global warming.

OZONE DEPLETION, THE VIENNA CONVENTION, AND THE MONTREAL PROTOCOL

We noted in Chapter 4 that ozone in the upper atmosphere is a valuable compound that tends to reduce the amount of ultraviolet radiation that reaches the earth's surface. The ozone layer, as it is called, protects the earth's inhabitants from skin cancer and cataracts. Over time, emissions of ozone-depleting substances (ODSs), such as certain refrigerants, proved to be depleting the ozone layer. Once scientists reached a consensus on the issue, the international community moved quickly to design a legal regime to address the problem. Strongly in support of the movement was the American chemical industry, which saw a business opportunity to manufacture substitutes for ozone-depleting chemicals.

The first step in the process was the Vienna Convention. This treaty is set in the form of a *framework convention*.

This means that the treaty itself does not contain specific obligations that require action on the part of the parties. Rather, it sets up a procedure by which parties agree to develop binding obligations later, over time, in a protocol or series of protocols to the original framework treaty. The Vienna Convention was negotiated primarily by wealthy countries, with poor and developing nations (the so-called *global South*) coming on board later.

The key protocol to the Vienna Convention that implemented reductions in the use of ozone-depleting chemicals was the Montreal Protocol on Substances that Deplete the Ozone Layer. Under that protocol and amendments that followed it, ODSs are phased out over a relatively short period of time. The U.S. Senate promptly ratified the treaty. The Congress then enacted implementing legislation, amending the Tax Code and the Clean Air Act.

The Montreal Protocol has been ratified by most of the global community. It has been quite successful, both domestically and around the globe, at reducing the use of ODSs.

GLOBAL WARMING, THE FRAMEWORK CONVENTION FOR CLIMATE CHANGE, AND THE KYOTO PROTOCOL

The problem of global warming was also described in Chapter 4. Greenhouse gases (GHGs) — including, most notably, carbon-based gases — move to the upper atmosphere, where they tend to act as a shield that keeps heat from the sun from radiating back out into space. The effect of accumulating GHGs is to raise temperatures around the globe. The place from which an emission of a GHG originates is irrelevant to the effect. However, this increase in temperature will have different effects around the globe. Some areas could accept a temperature increase without much negative effect. In other areas, a temperature increase may result in disease — from increases in disease-carrying insects, for example. Also, as temperatures rise, water levels rise as well; this may result in some land areas disappearing under the oceans.

International treatment of global warming proceeded, in some ways, parallel to the treatment of ozone depletion. In other ways, the two situations diverge. From the beginning, many political actors — who negotiate treaties — were less sanguine about the consensus of the scientific community on the matter. The first international agreement on global warming was, as with ozone-depleting chemicals, a framework convention. Indeed, it is called the Framework Convention on Climate Change (FCCC).

To date, the important protocol under the FCCC is the Kyoto Protocol. The protocol breaks parties down into developed countries, countries with transition economies (essentially the former Soviet Union), and developing countries. Developed countries and transition economies are called on to adjust their greenhouse gas emissions to a percentage of their 1990 levels; in most cases, this adjustment is a reduction. Developing countries are not called on to make any reductions.

Largely as the result of U.S. presence in the negotiations, the protocol contemplates emissions trading. First, developed countries are invited to trade emissions rights among one another. Second, under a device called *joint implementation*, entities from developed countries and transition economies can work together on projects that reduce GHG emissions and thereby generate GHG emissions credits. Finally, under a device called the *clean development mechanism*, actors in developed countries may engage in a project in developing countries. If the project is certified to reduce net GHG emissions, then the actor in the developed country gets emissions credits that it may use or sell.

As previously noted, the United States was heavily involved in the negotiation of the Kyoto Protocol. The protocol was never submitted to the Senate for ratification, however. Indeed, the Senate was nearly unanimous in expressing its sentiment against the protocol. The basis for this opposition seems to have been a sense that developing countries were not being asked to shoulder their fair share of GHG reductions (combined perhaps with some unexpressed skepticism over the science of global warming).

The Kyoto Protocol took effect in 2005 when Russia ratified it. It remains unclear whether the United States will ratify the protocol or its successor in whatever form it may take.

THE RELEVANCE OF DOMESTIC LAW

To this point, we have focused on international law. Is domestic law relevant to international law? It is, in at least four ways.

First, domestic legislation is required to implement an international environmental law treaty. As mentioned earlier, Congress passed legislation — under the Tax Code and the Clean Air Act — to implement the Montreal Protocol's phase out of ODSs. Another example is implementation of the trade restrictions under the Convention on International Trade in Endangered Species as part of the domestic Endangered Species Act.

Second, domestic laws may be used to address international environmental challenges even if there is no treaty or implementing legislation on the books. For example, the Supreme Court in *Massachusetts v. EPA*[2] rejected EPA's argument that it lacked authority to regulate greenhouse gas emissions from motor vehicles and constrained the grounds on which EPA could justifiably decline to exercise that authority. A 2008 Ninth Circuit decision[3] followed up on the *Massachusetts* case to hold that the National Highway Traffic Safety Administration had to consider the effects of global warming in setting motor vehicle fleet fuel economy standards.

Third, the first Congress enacted a law — called the Alien Tort Statute (ATS) — that allows aliens to bring suit in U.S. federal courts alleging violations of international law. A few cases have considered claims of violations of the rights of citizens in other countries to a healthy environment — framed as a right under customary international law. The federal courts have rejected these claims on the ground that no clear customary international law right yet exists.

Fourth, consider the problem of applying U.S. domestic environmental laws extraterritorially. Many environmentally minded individuals support this idea, because U.S. environmental laws are often more protective than their counterparts around the globe. However, the application of U.S. laws abroad raises important concerns. If the United States can legislate globally, what about the sovereignty of other nations? More generally, if every nation's environmental laws applied everywhere, wouldn't the country with the most protective laws have the only laws that mattered?

U.S. courts have considered the extraterritorial effect of the U.S. environmental laws and reached different conclusions. Extraterritorial application of the National Environmental Policy Act (NEPA) has been upheld on the ground that the decision-making process to which NEPA is directed is always domestic, even if the effect of the relevant decision may ultimately be felt abroad.[4] The Ninth Circuit has held that the Comprehensive Environmental Response, Compensation, and Liability Act (CERCLA) applies extraterritorially to a factory in British Columbia, Canada, where hazardous waste from the plant comes to rest in Washington State.[5] On the other hand, the same court has also denied extraterritorial effect to CERCLA when the polluted site is in a foreign country on what used to be (but is no longer) a U.S. military base.[6]

Note also that the U.S. Congress has conferred certain extraterritorial benefits on other countries under the U.S. environmental laws. The Clean Air Act, for example, gives a foreign government the power to ask EPA to issue a SIP call with respect to emissions from a state that causes dangerous air pollution conditions in the foreign nation, provided that the foreign country gives the United States "essentially the same rights."[7]

The U.S. courts are not the only tribunals called on to determine the proper extraterritorial effect of U.S. environmental laws. The World Trade Organization (WTO) Appellate Body is an international tribunal that hears claims by one nation (or group of nations) that actions by another nation are in violation of the General Agreement on Tariffs and Trade (GATT), a collection of trade treaties. The Appellate Body has invalidated a U.S. statute that sought to require catchers of shrimp in foreign countries to use particular "turtle-exclusion devices" designed to spare an endangered sea turtle that is otherwise put at risk by shrimp harvesting. The Appellate Body concluded that the United States had failed to exhaust diplomatic options, as required under the GATT. Some commentators believe that the WTO Appellate Body is tilted in favor of trade and economic growth over environmental concerns. Others see the Appellate Body's decisions, including the shrimp-turtle decision, as not being entirely antienvironment and as sowing the seeds for a viable environmentally friendly jurisprudence.

CHAPTER RECAP

What have we learned in this chapter? To the extent that international environmental law is in effect, it tends to come in the form of bilateral and multilateral treaty regimes. Because entry into a treaty regime is voluntary, the regimes must be constructed in a way so as to encourage entry and discourage exit. This can prove to be difficult.

One great success story is the international agreement to phase out the production and use of ozone-depleting substances. Action was taken quickly after scientific consensus coalesced about the problem, enrollment in the regime was robust, and tangible results followed soon after. In contrast, the regime to control emissions of greenhouse gases has been less successful. More countries have questioned the underlying science, and not as many countries have entered the regime. Moreover, many argue that the existing regime would not be sufficient to deal with the problem even if all countries were to come on board.

ENDNOTES

1. *Jus cogens* is another possible source of international law. This includes fundamental norms of international behavior. *Jus cogens* differs from customary international law in that it is not possible for a nation to take steps affirmatively to excuse itself from compliance with *jus cogens*.

2. 549 U.S. 497 (2007)

3. *Center for Biological Diversity v. National Highway Traffic Safety Admin.*, 538 F.3d 1172 (9th Cir. 2008).

4. *See Environmental Defense Fund, Inc. v. Massey*, 986 F.2d 528 (D.C. Cir. 1993).

5. *See Pakootas v. Teck Cominco Metals, Ltd.*, 452 F.3d 1066 (9th Cir. 2006).

6. *See ARC Ecology v. U.S. Dep't of the Air Force*, 411 F.3d 1092 (9th Cir. 2005).

7. Clean Air Act §115, 42 U.S.C. §7415.

Glossary

Action agency. Under the Endangered Species Act (ESA) regulations, agency that is undertaking action that is "likely to jeopardize the continued existence of any species proposed to be listed under the ESA or result in the destruction or adverse modification of critical habitat proposed to be designated for such species," and therefore must consult with the relevant expert agency. Discussed on page 122.

Administrative Procedure Act (APA). Federal statute that governs the promulgation of, and challenges to, agency regulations. Discussed on pages 46–47, 146–147.

Anthropocentric justifications for environmental protection and regulation. Justifications for environmental protection and regulation that are based on human utility, wants, needs, and perceptions. Discussed on pages 2, 9.

Anticipatory nuisance doctrine. Under the common law of nuisance, doctrine generally disfavoring nuisance actions based on anticipation on harm, before actual interference with property rights have actually occurred. Discussed on page 12.

Applicable, relevant and appropriate requirements (ARAR). The "applicable or relevant and appropriate" standards with which the Comprehensive Environmental Response, Compensation, and Liability Act cleanups must comply. Discussed on page 104.

Army Corps of Engineers. Agency that fulfills the Secretary of the Army's obligations under the Clean Water Act's Section 404 wetlands protection program. Discussed on pages 14, 90.

Arranger. Category of potentially responsible party that generates hazardous substances and sends those substances to treatment and disposal facilities, or that sends hazardous substances to another actor with the intent that the other actor dispose of at least a portion of the hazardous substances. Also called *generator*.

Attainment. An area that is in compliance with the national ambient air quality standards. Discussed on page 59.

Best available control technology (BACT). Under the Clean Air Act: Standard with which new major emitting facilities in prevention of significant deterioration areas must comply. Discussed on page 60.

Under the Clean Water Act: Standard of performance applicable to new sources. Discussed on page 83.

Best available technology economically achievable (BAT). Effluent standard under the Clean Water Act applicable to nonconventional pollutants discharged by point sources. Discussed on pages 82–83.

Best conventional technology (BCT). Effluent standard under the Clean Water Act applicable to conventional pollutants discharged by point sources. Discussed on pages 82–83.

Best management practices (BMP). Management practices that states are called upon under the Clean Water Act to adopt for nonpoint sources of water pollution. Discussed on pages 84–85.

Best practicable control technology (BPT). Effluent standard under the Clean Water Act with which the original Clean Water Act called upon point source dischargers of nontoxic pollutants to comply. Discussed on page 82.

Biological opinion. Under the Endangered Species Act, opinion that must be prepared if a government action may adversely affect a listed species or critical habitat; it assesses whether the action in question is likely to adversely affect the listed species or critical habitat. Discussed on pages 122–123.

Bubble program. The Environmental Protection Agency regulation under the Clean Air Act's prevention of significant deterioration program that interprets the statutory word *source* to allow operators of stationary sources to offset increased emissions from a new facility against reductions in air emissions from an existing outlet at the same facility. Discussed on page 61.

Characteristic hazardous waste. A waste that is hazardous by virtue of the fact that it exhibits one of four characteristics: ignitability, corrosivity, reactivity, or toxicity. Discussed on pages 99–100.

***Chevron* test.** Drawing its name from the Supreme Court's opinion in *Chevron U.S.A. v. Natural Resources Defense Council*, test that courts use to assess whether or not an agency's interpretation of a statute is deserving of judicial deference. Discussed on pages 47–48.

Clean Air Act. Major federal statute designed to address and ameliorate air pollution. Discussed in Chapter 3.

Clean Water Act. Major federal statute designed to address and ameliorate water pollution. Discussed in Chapter 4.

Climate change. *See* global warming.

Command-and-control regime. A form of environmental regulation that involves the government issuing mandates with which regulated actors must comply. Discussed on pages 18–19.

Commerce Clause. Constitutional provision that provides the Congress with power to regulate interstate and international commerce. Discussed on pages 36–37.

Comprehensive Emergency Response, Compensation and Liability Act (CERCLA). Federal statute designed to address, and arrange financial coverage for, cleanups of releases of hazardous substances. Discussed on pages 102–113.

Continuous emissions monitoring system. System that keeps track of pollution emissions on an ongoing basis, installation of which is required under the Clean Air Act's national sulfur dioxide emissions allowance trading program. Discussed on page 27.

Cooperative federalism. Overarching theory under which the federal and state governments work together to achieve regulatory goals. Discussed on pages 20–24, 33.

Corporate average fuel economy (CAFE) standards. Under the Energy Policy and Conservation Act, the mandated average motor vehicle fuel economy standards — that is, miles the vehicle can travel per gallon of gasoline — for a manufacturer's fleets of motor vehicles. Discussed on pages 70–71.

Cost-benefit analysis. Process for government decision making, under which a program is undertaken when the benefits of the program outweigh the costs. Discussed on pages 7–9.

Cost-effectiveness. Process for government decision making, under a choice among possible programs is made based on which program provides the greatest surplus of benefits over costs. Discussed on pages 7–8.

Council on Environmental Quality (CEQ). White House agency that issues regulations on the application of the National Environmental Policy Act. Discussed on pages 131–136, 138.

Criteria pollutant. Air pollutant the emission of which, in the Environmental Protection Agency's (EPA) judgment, "may reasonably be anticipated to endanger public health or welfare." EPA must issue national ambient air quality standards for criteria pollutants. Discussed on page 56.

Customary international law. International law that arises when the nations of the world observe the legal principle at issue. Discussed on page 158.

Delisting. Under the Endangered Species Act, the removal of a species from the list of endangered and threatened species. Discussed on page 120.

Derived-from rule. Environmental Protection Agency regulation under the Comprehensive Environmental Response, Compensation, and Liability Act, under which a substance derived from the treatment, storage, or disposal of a listed hazardous waste is deemed itself to be hazardous. Discussed on page 100.

Designated use. Part of water quality standard that defines the use to which the water body (or segment thereof) is to be put. Discussed on pages 85–86.

Dormant Commerce Clause. Judicial interpretation of the U.S. Constitution's Commerce Clause that disables states from regulating in certain areas that are asecondОКOKOK.

seen to impinge upon interstate commerce, absent congressional authorization. Discussed on pages 37–38.

Downlisting. Under the Endangered Species Act, the migration of a species from the list of endangered species to the list of threatened species. Discussed on page 120.

Emergency Planning and Community Right-to-Know Act (EPCRA). Federal statute that mandates that polluters disclose discharges of toxic pollutants under the toxic release inventory. Discussed on pages 114, 140.

Eminent domain. Power of government, implicit in the U.S. Constitution's Takings Clause, that takes private property for public use. Discussed on page 41.

Emission allowance. A tradable pollution permit under the Clean Air Act's sulfur dioxide emission allowance trading program that allows its holder to emit one ton of sulfur dioxide in one calendar year. Discussed on page 65.

Endangered species. Under the Endangered Species Act, a species that is "in danger of extinction throughout all or a significant portion of its range." Discussed on page 118.

Endangered Species Act (ESA). Federal statute designed to protect endangered and threatened species. Discussed in Chapter 6.

End-of-pipe regulation. Regulation that limits those who generate the pollution based on their pollution output. Discussed on pages 15, 27.

Energy Policy and Conservation Act (EPCA). Federal statute that mandates corporate average fuel economy standards for fleets of motor vehicles. Discussed on pages 70–71.

Environmental assessment (EA). An abbreviated environmental impact statement that is prepared in order to support a "finding of no significant impact." Discussed on pages 132, 136–137, 141.

Environmental impact statement (EIS). A document prepared under the National Environmental Policy Act that evaluates the environmental impact of a major federal action. Discussed on pages 129–141.

Environmental Protection Agency (EPA). Federal agency with primary responsibility for interpretation and enforcement of most federal environmental laws. Discussed initially on page 14.

Expert agency. Under Endangered Species Act regulations, as between the Fish and Wildlife Service and the National Marine Fisheries Service, the agency with responsibility for the endangered or threatened species at issue. Discussed on page 122.

Externality. Cost (or benefit) that an actor does not take account of, but rather passes on to someone else. Uncompensated pollution harm that a factory passes on to individuals living nearby is an example of a *negative externality*; the benefit that a homeowner enjoys by virtue of a beautiful garden on adjoining land is an example of a *positive externality*. Discussed on pages 5, 7, 9, 24.

Federal floor. Federal standard for environmental protection that states are free to exceed, but not reduce. Discussed on pages 21–22.

Federal implementation plan (FIP). Plan that the federal government may impose when a state implementation plan (SIP) is inadequate, and the state fails adequately to respond to a SIP call. Discussed on page 58.

Federal Insecticide, Fungicide, and Rodenticide Act (FIFRA). Federal statute that regulates the production and sale of insecticides, fungicides, and rodenticides. Discussed on pages 39, 113, 147.

Finding of no significant impact (FONSI). A finding that a major federal action will *not* give rise to a significant environmental impact, thus obviating the need to prepare an environmental impact statement. Discussed on pages 132, 137, 141.

Fish and Wildlife Service (FWS). Agency within the Department of the Interior that shares responsibility along with the National Marine Fisheries Service for administering the Endangered Species Act. Discussed on pages 14, 118–123, 126–127.

Framework Convention for Climate Change (FCCC). Initial international treaty designed to address global warming. Discussed on pages 160–161.

Free rider. One who does not contribute to a cause, expecting that he or she will benefit from the cause once others contribute to it. Discussed on page 11.

General Agreement on Tariffs and Trade (GATT). A collection of international trade treaties. Discussed on page 164.

Generator. Societal actors, subject to regulation under the Resource Conservation and Recovery Act, generate hazardous wastes. Discussed on page 101.

Another name for the "arranger" category of potentially responsible party under the Comprehensive Environmental Response, Compensation, and Liability Act.

Global warming. Phenomenon caused by greenhouse gases in the atmosphere that leads to increases in temperatures and, concomitantly, sea level rise and increases in extreme weather conditions. Also referred to as *climate change*. Discussed on pages 1, 11, 53, 56, 71, 152, 159–162.

God Squad. A committee consisting of seven members: the secretaries of agriculture, of the interior, and of the Army; the chair of the President's Council of Economic Advisers; the Environmental Protection Agency Administrator; the administrator of the National Oceanic and Atmospheric Administration; and a representative from the affected state appointed by the president; so named because of its power to exempt particular projects from the Endangered Species Act coverage and thus to determine the fate of endangered and threatened species. Discussed on page 124.

Grandfathering. Notion that pollution sources that predate enactment or issuance of an environmental regulation are subject to less stringent regulation than are new or modified sources. Discussed on pages 62–63.

Greenhouse gases (GHGs). Gases that contribute to the climate change, or global warming. Discussed on pages 12, 53–54, 56, 69, 72, 148, 152, 160–162, 165.

Habitat conservation plan (HCP). Under the Endangered Species Act, a prerequisite to an incidental take permit; it must specify (1) the likely impact of the taking of the species in question that would be authorized, (2) steps the applicant will undertake to minimize and mitigate that impact, and (3) possible alternatives that the applicant considered and the reasons why those alternatives were not chosen. Discussed on page 126.

Hazardous air pollutant (HAPs). Air pollutants listed by Congress under the Clean Air Act as hazardous to human health. Discussed on pages 63–64.

Hazardous substance. Subject of regulation under the Comprehensive Environmental Response, Compensation, and Liability Act; defined to include hazardous wastes as defined under the Resource Conservation and Recovery Act, hazardous air pollutants as defined under the Clean Air Act, and toxic water pollutants as defined under the Clean Water Act, but excludes petroleum and natural gas. Discussed on page 103.

Hazardous waste. Solid wastes that qualify as hazardous under the Resource Conservation and Recovery Act, either because they are on a list of hazardous wastes or because they exhibit one of four hazardous characteristics: ignitability, corrosivity, reactivity, or toxicity. Discussed on pages 99–100.

Incidental take permit (ITP). A permit authorizes an action that the Endangered Species Act would otherwise prohibit because of harm to a listed species; it is available only if the authorized take is "incidental to, and not the purpose of, the carrying out of an otherwise lawful activity." Discussed on pages 126–127.

Incidental take statement (ITS). Under the Endangered Species Act, a statement provided by either the Fish and Wildlife Service or the National Marine Fisheries Service that authorizes a federal action that may have an incidental effect on a listed species and that, among other things, sets out terms and conditions with which the federal agency (or applicant) must comply and specifies "the procedures to be used to handle or dispose of any individuals of a species actually taken." Discussed on page 123.

Interconnectedness of the environmental system. Notion that, because, ultimately, the Earth is a unified system, what may seem at first to be a small effect on one small aspect of that system may in the end throw the entire system into disarray. Discussed on page 3.

Jeopardy opinion. Opinion issued by the Fish and Wildlife Service or National Marine Fisheries Service that a government action, taken together with cumulative effects, is likely to jeopardize the continued existence of listed species or result in the destruction or adverse modification of critical habitat. Discussed on page 123.

Just compensation. Amount that the U.S. Constitution mandates that an owner of property be compensated when his or her property is "taken" by the government. Discussed on page 41.

Kyoto Protocol. International treaty that follows up on the Framework Convention on Climate Change; sets targets to reduce greenhouse gas emissions. Discussed on pages 72, 161–162.

Listed hazardous waste. Waste that is hazardous because it appears on a list of hazardous wastes. Discussed on page 99.

Listed species. An endangered or threatened species listed as such under the Endangered Species Act. Discussed on pages 118, 120–123, 126.

Lowest achievable emission rate (LAER). Under the Clean Air Act, the standard with which new and modified stationary sources in nonattainment areas must comply. Discussed on pages 59–60.

Market-based regime. A form of environmental regulation that involves the government setting one aspect of regulation, but leaving regulated actors free to decide how to comply with the regulation. Discussed on pages 18–19.

Maximum contaminant level (MCL). Under the Solid Waste Disposal Act, a standard set for a drinking water contaminant that is to be set as close to the maximum contaminant level goal as is feasible. Discussed on pages 92–93.

Maximum contaminant level goal (MCLG). Under the Solid Waste Disposal Act, for a given drinking water contaminant, "the level at which no known or anticipated adverse effects on the health of persons occur and which allows an adequate margin of safety." Discussed on page 92.

Mixture rule. Environmental Protection Agency regulation under the Comprehensive Environmental Response, Compensation, and Liability Act, under which a mixture of a characteristic hazardous waste with another substance is itself deemed to be hazardous. Discussed on page 100.

Mobile source. An air pollution source that moves, such as a motor vehicle. Discussed on pages 55, 69–70.

Montreal Protocol. Primary international treaty that follows up on the Vienna Convention and seeks to implement phaseout of ozone-depleting substances. Discussed on pages 159–160, 162.

Narrative criteria. Water quality criteria expressed in narrative form. Discussed on page 86.

National ambient air quality standard (NAAQS). Ambient air quality level set by the Environmental Protection Agency under the Clean Air Act for each criteria pollutant in order to protect human health and welfare. Discussed on pages 55–59, 61, 66–67, 71, 86.

National Environmental Policy Act (NEPA). Federal statute designed to require consideration of environmental impacts in government decision making. Discussed in Chapter 7.

National Highway Traffic Safety Administration (NHTSA). Agency within the Department of Transportation with authority to promulgate corporate average fuel economy standards under the Energy Policy and Conservation Act. Discussed on pages 14, 70–71.

National Marine Fisheries Service (NMFS). Agency within the Department of the Commerce's National Oceanic and Atmospheric Administration that shares responsibility along with the Fish and Wildlife Service for administering the Endangered Species Act. Discussed on pages 14, 52, 118–123, 126–127.

National pollutant discharge elimination system (NPDES). Clean Water Act program designed to permit point source dischargers of water pollutants. Discussed on pages 80, 93.

National Priority List (NPL). Under Comprehensive Environmental Response, Compensation, and Liability Act, list of sites that, by virtue of know or threatened releases of hazardous substances, are most seriously contaminated and most warrant cleanup. Discussed on page 103.

New source performance standards (NSPS). Under the Clean Air Act, standards with which new and modified stationary sources must comply. Discussed on pages 62, 68.

New source review. Notion under the Clean Air Act, which new and modified sources are subject to more stringent environmental regulation than are preexisting sources. Discussed on pages 59–61, 61–63, 71.

No jeopardy opinion. Opinion issued by the Fish and Wildlife Service or National Marine Fisheries Service that an action by the government (or the implementation of any reasonable and prudent alternatives) will result only in "incidental take of listed species," and accordingly will not violate the Endangered Species Act. Discussed on page 123.

Nonpoint source. Under the Clean Water Act, water pollution source other than a point source; as compared to point sources, they are largely unregulated. Discussed on pages 79, 84, 87–88, 93.

Nuisance. Common law doctrine under which a property owner may sue a neighboring property owner for interference with enjoyment of his or her property. Discussed on pages 10–12, 33.

Office of Information and Regulatory Affairs (OIRA). Office within the Office of Management and Budget that reviews regulations for compliance with executive orders. Discussed on page 46.

Office of Management and Budget (OMB). Office within the White House charged with, among other things, review of regulations before they are issued. Discussed on page 46.

Ozone-depleting substance (ODS). A substance that contributes to depletion of the ozone layer. Discussed on pages 159–160, 162.

Ozone depletion. International environmental challenge involving the reduction of the atmospheric ozone layer that shields the Earth's surface from harmful solar radiation, and thus protects humans from skin cancer and glaucoma. Discussed on pages 159–160, 162, 164–165.

Pigouvian tax. Named for economist Arthur Pigou, an environmental tax that is set at an amount exactly equal to the marginal harm caused by each pollution emission. Discussed on pages 15–16.

Point source. Under the Clean Water Act, essentially, sources of water pollution that take the form of a readily identifiable point, such as a pipe, ditch, or conduit; they are subject to substantial regulation under the act. Discussed on pages 78–79.

Polluter pays principle. Normative principle of environmental law, and perhaps principle of customary international law, that calls for polluters to pay for ameliorating, and for harms resulting from, their pollution. Discussed on pages 14, 158.

Potentially responsible party (PRP). Party potentially responsible for cleanup costs under the Comprehensive Environmental Response, Compensation, and Liability Act. Discussed on pages 105–111, 114.

Precautionary principle. Normative principle of environmental law, and perhaps principle of customary international law, that calls for precaution in the face of uncertainty. Discussed on pages 3, 15, 92, 158.

Preemption of state law. Displacement of state law by federal law. Discussed on pages 39–40.

Prevention of significant deterioration (PSD). Clean Air Act program designed to protect pristine air quality in areas in which ambient air quality exceeds the levels required by the national ambient air quality standards. Discussed on pages 60–61, 63, 68, 71.

Race to the bottom. Paradigmatic account under which jurisdictions bid down the level of environmental protection in order to compete for businesses to locate within their borders. Discussed on pages 22, 24.

Reasonably available control measures (RACM). Under the Clean Air Act, measures called for in nonattainment areas. Discussed on page 59.

Reasonably available control technology (RACT). Under the Clean Air Act, standard with which existing sources in nonattainment areas must comply. Discussed on page 59.

Regulatory taking. A regulation that, while it does not appropriate private property, so restricts the private property owner's rights that it gives rise to a government obligation to compensate the property owner. Discussed on pages 41–45.

Resource Conservation and Recovery Act (RCRA). Federal statute designed to monitor and control generation; transportation; and treatment, storage, and disposal of hazardous wastes. Discussed on page 98–102.

Safe Drinking Water Act (SDWA). Federal act designed to protect the safety of drinking water. Discussed on pages 92–93.

Solid waste. Defined under the Solid Waste Disposal Act as "any garbage, refuse, sludge from a waste treatment plant, water supply treatment plant, or air pollution control facility and other discarded material, including solid, liquid, semisolid, or contained gaseous material resulting from industrial, commercial, mining, and agricultural operations, and from community activities." Discussed on pages 98–99.

Solid Waste Disposal Act (SWDA). Federal act designed to regulate the treatment and disposal of solid wastes. Discussed on pages 98–99, 115.

State implementation plan (SIP). Plan generated by state under the Clean Air Act that explains how the state will attain the national ambient air quality standards. Discussed on pages 57–59, 66–69.

Stationary source. A nonmoving source of air pollution. Discussed on pages 58–60, 62–64, 67–68.

Sulfur dioxide emission allowance. Issued under the Clean Air Act's national sulfur dioxide emission allowance trading program, a statutory authorization that authorizes its holder to emit one ton of sulfur dioxide in the course of a calendar year. Discussed on pages 64–66.

Sulfur dioxide emission allowance trading program. Clean Air Act program that caps the total annual amount of sulfur dioxide emissions, and distributes the authorizations to emit that amount in the form of tradable pollution permits (called *emission allowances*). Discussed on pages 64–66.

Supremacy Clause. Constitutional provision that establishes that federal constitutional law, statutory law, and treaties trump inconsistent state laws. Discussed on pages 39–40, 51.

Takings Clause. Constitutional provision that requires government to pay "just compensation" to private property owners whose property is taken by the government. Discussed on pages 41–45, 51.

Tax-based regime. Regulatory regime that employs taxes to achieve an environmental regulatory goal. Discussed on pages 15–19.

Threatened species. Under the Endangered Species Act, a species that is "likely to become an endangered species in the foreseeable future throughout all or a significant portion of its range." Discussed on page 118.

Total maximum daily load (TMDL) standard. Under the Clean Water Act, promulgated by the state with respect to water bodies (or segments thereof) for which the effluent limitations of the National Pollutant Discharge Elimination System permits issued for polluters who discharge pollution into the relevant water body are insufficient to allow attainment of the relevant water quality standards; amount of pollutant in question that can acceptably enter the water body on a daily basis, while still allowing for attainment of the relevant water quality standard. Discussed on page 87.

Toxic pollutants. Under the Clean Water Act, water pollutants that threaten human health (including carcinogens). Discussed on pages 82–83.

Toxic release inventory (TRI). Inventory assembled from disclosures, mandated under the Emergency Planning and Community Right-to-Know Aact, of releases of toxic chemicals. Discussed on pages 114, 140.

Toxic Substances Control Act (TSCA). Federal statute that regulates dangerous chemicals and requires testing of new products. Discussed on page 113.

Toxic tort. Common law tort claims, often brought as class actions, that seek to vindicate the rights of those harmed by toxic substances. Discussed on pages 11–12, 20–21.

Tradable pollution permit regime. Regulatory regime that proceeds by capping the amount of acceptable pollutant emissions over a given period of time (often annually), then divides that amount among emission permits, then distributes those permits to societal actors and allows them to be traded. Discussed on pages 16–18.

Transporter. Societal actors, subject to regulation under the Resource Conservation and Recovery Act, that transport hazardous wastes. Discussed on page 101.

Under the Comprehensive Environmental Response, Compensation, and Liability Act, a category of potentially responsible party by virtue of the fact that he or she "accepts or accepted any hazardous substances for transport to disposal or treatment facilities, incineration vessels or sites selected by such person." Discussed on page 108.

Treatment, storage, and disposal facilities (TSDFs). Facilities, subject to regulation under the Resource Conservation and Recovery Act, that treat, store, and dispose of hazardous wastes. Discussed on page 101.

Unitary federal choice. A federal environmental standard that preempts state law in its entirety. Discussed on page 23.

Vienna Convention. Initial international treaty designed to combat ozone depletion. Discussed on pages 159–160.

Water quality criteria. Part of a water quality standard that sets the maximum level of the relevant pollutant appropriate to accommodate the chosen designated use. Discussed on pages 85–86.

Water quality standard. Standard that the Clean Water Act calls upon states to set for water segments within their borders. Consists of designated use and water quality standard. Discussed on pages 85–88.

World Trade Organization (WTO). International organization that administers the General Agreement on Tariffs and Trade. Discussed on page 164.

Index